Number Bonds Fun

Photocopiable activities for practising number bonds
Activities for Years 1 & 2

Original concept, design and content by
Mark & Katy Hill

Cover illustration by
Julie Anderson
with
Darcy Bell-Myers & Terri Moll

Inside illustrations by
Julie Anderson

LDA

Copyright Notice

This book contains worksheets which may be reproduced by photocopier or other means for use by the purchaser. This book and all its contents remain copyright. Copies may be made from these masters without reference to the publisher or to the licensing scheme for the making of photocopies operated by the Publishers Licensing Agency.

The rights of Mark and Katy Hill to be identified as the authors of this work have been asserted by them in accordance with sections 77 and 78 of the Copyright, Designs and Patents Act 1988.

Number Bonds Fun
MT00488
ISBN-13: 978 1 85503 315 3
© Mark and Katy Hill
All rights reserved

First published 2001
Reprinted 2002, 2004, 2005 (twice), 2007, 2010, 2012, 2013, 2014, 2015, 2016

Printed in the UK for LDA
Pintail Close, Victoria Business Park, Nottingham, NG4 2SG, UK

Table of Contents

Instructions 4
Individual Education Plan targets 8
Notes 9
Number 5 bonds 10
Number 6 bonds 15
Number 7 bonds 20
Number 8 bonds 25
Number 9 bonds 30
Number 10 bonds 35
Number 11 bonds 52
Number 12 bonds 54
Number 13 bonds 56
Number 14 bonds 58
Number 15 bonds 60
Number 16 bonds 62
Number 17 bonds 64
Number 18 bonds 66
Number 19 bonds 68
Number 20 bonds 70
Number 50 bonds 79
Number 100 bonds 82
Mixed number bonds 89

© *Number Bonds Fun* LDA

Instructions

Activity 1 Number bond mice
Children follow the mice to the computers to find the number 5 bond pairs. Children colour the mice and computer pair the same colour and then write the bond pairs on the reverse of the sheet.

Activity 2 Weather bonds
Children look/say/cover/write/check the number 5 bond pairs. They then colour each bond pair a different colour.

Activity 3 Buckets and spades
Children colour match the bucket with its spade partner to make number 5 bond pairs.

Activity 4 Number bond towers
Children choose a coloured pencil and colour the blocks in each tower specified by the number below it. This will build a staircase pattern. The children should notice how many blocks are coloured and how many blocks are not coloured in each tower to see the number bond pattern.

Activity 5 Number bond dice
Children identify the dice pairs that score five. Colour these blue and other dice pairs green.

Activity 6 Dogs and leads
Children follow the leads to the dogs to find the number 6 bond pairs. Children colour the lead and dog pairs the same colour and then write the bond pairs on the reverse of the sheet.

Activity 7 Caterpillars and leaves
Children look/say/cover/write/check the number 6 bond pairs. They then colour each bond pair a different colour.

Activity 8 Crabs and shells
Children colour match the crabs with their shell partners to make number 6 bond pairs.

Activity 9 Number bond trains
Children choose two different coloured pencils. They use the number 6 bond pairs in each engine to help colour the carriages. For example, 2/4 means colour two carriages red and four green.

Activity 10 What's on the line?
Draw the children's attention to six items of washing on every line. On each line count the number of socks and the number of hankies. Can the children write the bond pairs on the reverse of the sheet and re-order the bond pairs created?

Activity 11 Number bond balloons
Children follow the balloon strings to the labels to find the number 7 bond pairs. Children colour the balloon and the box the same colour and then write the bond pairs on the reverse of the sheet.

Activity 12 Cakes and cherries
Children look/say/cover/write/check the number 7 bond pairs. They then colour each bond pair a different colour.

Activity 13 Bows and arrows
Children colour match each bow with its arrow partner to make number 7 bond pairs.

Activity 14 Sailing boat number bonds
Children calculate the number bond pairs. Those that total seven are coloured yellow. All other totals can be coloured red.

Activity 15 Crowns
Each crown is topped with 7 small jewels. Children choose two different colours and colour these jewels according to the number seven bonds given inside each crown.

Activity 16 Yo-Yos
Children follow the yo-yo strings to the finger loops to find the number 8 bond pairs. Children colour the yo-yo and finger loop pairs the same colour and then write the bond pairs on the reverse of the sheet.

Activity 17 Ice-cream and lollies
Children look/say/cover/write/check the number 8 bond pairs. They then colour each bond pair a different colour.

Activity 18 Keys to the door
Children colour match the key with its door partner to make number 8 bond pairs.

Activity 19 Flags
Children choose two different coloured pencils and colour the flags to show the number 8 bond pairs. Encourage the children to colour starting on the top left each time so that their colouring shows a pattern.

Activity 20 Dominoes
Children identify the dominoes that score eight. Colour these red and other dominoes green.

Activity 21 Kites
Children follow the kite strings to the handles to find the number 9 bond pairs. Children colour the kite and handle pairs the same colour then write the bond pairs on the reverse of the sheet.

Activity 22 Presents and bows
Children look/say/cover/write/check the number 9 bond pairs. They then colour each bond pair a different colour.

Activity 23 Bottles of shampoo
Children colour match the bubbles with their bottle partners to make number 9 bond pairs.

Activity 24 Number bond necklaces

Children choose two different coloured pencils and colour the necklaces according to the number 9 bond pairs. Encourage the children to begin colouring from the left. This will give a coloured staircase.

Activity 25 Suitcases

Children identify the suitcases containing pairs that total nine. Colour these orange and the other suitcases blue.

Activity 26 Spaghetti and meatballs

Children follow the spaghetti from the meatball to the fork to find the number 10 bond pairs. Children colour the meatball and fork pair the same colour and then write the bond pairs on the reverse of the sheet.

Activity 27 Marbles and bags

Children look/say/cover/write/check the number 10 bond pairs. They then colour each bond pair a different colour.

Activity 28 Number bond balloons

Children colour match the balloons to make number 10 bond pairs.

Activity 29 Number bond memory rhyme

Children learn the number 10 bond pair memory rhyme. They can copy the rhyme or draw pictures in the space provided.

Activity 30 Number bond necklace search

Children find the hidden number bond pairs. Hidden pairs are adjoining numbers.

Activity 31 Apple trees

Each tree should have ten apples growing. However, some have fallen. Children use their knowledge of number 10 bond pairs to calculate how many should be remaining on the tree.

Activity 32 Number bond colour by numbers (1)

Children colour the picture by only colouring those shapes that contain a bond totalling 10.

Activity 33 Number bond colour by numbers (2)

Children colour the picture by only colouring those shapes that contain a number bond totalling 10.

Activity 34 Number bond search

Children find the number 10 bond pairs hiding in the grid. They are hidden vertically, horizontally and diagonally. The bonds are reproduced at the bottom of the page as an aid.

Activity 35 Christmas number bonds

Each Christmas bauble should contain a total of ten spots. The children are given the number of spots on the left-hand side. Can they calculate the number of missing spots and draw them in?

Activity 36 Number bond ladybirds

Each ladybird should contain a total of ten spots. The children are given the number of spots on the left-hand side. Can they calculate the number of missing spots and draw them in?

Activity 37 Ups and downs

Teach the children to use their fingers as an aid to number 10 bond calculations. *Fingers up* can represent one partner in the number bond pair and the *fingers down* can represent the other number bond partner. Use this sheet as a reinforcement to this teaching point or as an introduction.

Activity 38 Number bond snap cards
(Two sets–single digit cards and cards containing bond pairs.)

Photocopy, cut out and laminate two sets of these cards. They can then be used to play *Pelmanism pairs* where the children place them all face down and take turns to turn over a pair of cards. If the cards make a number 10 bond pair, e.g. 2 and 8, then the child has another go, otherwise play passes to their opponent.

Alternatively several sets can be copied and the children could use them to play *Snap* in the traditional way by playing in pairs. Cards are dealt face-down equally between the two playing children. Each child turns over a card from their own pile. If the cards total ten, then *Snap* is called. The child calling *Snap* first collects all the cards in the turned pile. If *Snap* is incorrectly called then the cards can be shared between face-down piles.

Activity 39 Number bond ruler drawing

Children use a ruler to join the points on the vertical and horizontal axes. The children should use the number bond pairs on the right of the worksheet as a key for joining from each axis. For instance, 1–9 means join number 1 on the horizontal axis to number 9 on the vertical axis.

Activity 40 Number bond pies

Children choose two different coloured pencils and colour the number bond pies according to the bond pairs beneath each pie. For instance, 9 and 1 means colour the pie with 9 pieces yellow and 1 piece orange. Encourage the children to begin colouring at the twelve o'clock position in each pie to create a pattern through the pies.

Activity 41 Can you crack the code?

Children work out the number 10 bond problem. Each answer in turn should be written in the next empty box at the foot of the page giving the hidden code when completed.

Code: 7 4 8 2 5 9 6 10 1 3 0

Activity 42 Going fishing
   Children colour match the fish with the hook partners to make number 11 bond pairs.

Activity 43 Magic carpet race
   Children to cut out the magic carpets and paste them in the correct order according to the number 11 bond pairs written on them. 11 and 0 comes first in the race followed by 10 and 1 and so on.

Activity 44 Stepping stones
   Children calculate the missing number 12 bonds on the left-hand side of the page. They then use these missing numbers to find their way across the stepping stones by colouring the correctly numbered stones.

Activity 45 Fish
   Children cut out the fish halves and paste the fish together by matching number 12 bond pairs.

Activity 46 Treasure island
   Children cut out each rectangle containing part of the treasure map. They then reassemble the map in its proper order by using their number 13 bonds.

Activity 47 Calculator number search
   Children find the number 13 bond pairs hidden in the calculator. They are given the bond pairs at the foot of the page as an aid and all bonds lie horizontally in the search grid.

Activity 48 Cherry tree
   Children to be given 14 interlocking cubes or counters. They then investigate different ways of partitioning 14 into two sub-sets, recording the bond partners in each cherry pair.

Activity 49 Birds' nests
   Children colour match the birds' eggs to their nests using their number 14 bonds.

Activity 50 Measuring number bonds
   Draw the children's attention to the fact that each strip measures 15 centimetres. The strips are divided into two pieces, each strip providing a number 15 bond pair. The children measure each part and record the length in the box.

Activity 51 Number bond rocket search
   Children find the number 15 bonds pairs hidden in the rocket. They are given the bond pairs at the foot of the page as an aid and all bonds lie vertically in the search grid.

Activity 52 Planet hopping
   Children calculate the missing number 16 bonds on the left-hand side of the page. They then use these missing numbers to find their way across the planets by colouring these missing numbers on the planets as they go.

Activity 53 Ticket machines
   Children colour match the tickets with the machine partners to make number 16 bond pairs.

Activity 54 Spinning plates
   Children identify the plates containing pairs that total 17. Colour these blue and the other plates green.

Activity 55 Hidden treasure
   Children calculate the missing number 17 bond partner. This will give the children the number of the square on the map grid where each item of treasure is to be found. Children draw each item of treasure in the correct square.

Activity 56 Farm number bond search
   Children find the number 18 bond pairs hidden in the cow. They are given the bond pairs on the right of the page as an aid. Pairs can be found diagonally.

Activity 57 Number bond pizzas
   Children to be given 18 interlocking cubes or counters. They then investigate different ways of partitioning 18 into two sub-sets, recording the bond partners in each pizza.

Activity 58 Bumble bees
   Children colour match the bees with their partners to make number 19 bond pairs.

Activity 59 Penalties
   Children identify the footballs containing number bond pairs that total 19. Colour these orange and the other footballs blue. Each correct answer scores a goal.

Activity 60 Purses
   Each purse should contain 20p but some money has fallen out. Can the children calculate the missing amounts from each purse **and** draw in the correct coin values?

Activity 61 Skipping ropes
   Children follow the ropes from one skipping rope handle to another to find the number 20 bond pairs. Children colour the handle pairs the same colour and then write the bond pairs on the reverse of the sheet.

Activity 62 Number bond bees lotto
(Two sheets—bees and flowers)
   Photocopy, decorate and laminate each sheet. Cut out the bees. The children then match each bee to its flower using their knowledge of the number 20 bond pairs. How quickly can they do this?

Activity 63 Spectacles
   Each pair of spectacles should contain a number 20 bond pair. Children calculate the missing bond partner. Colour each pair of spectacles a different colour. Children then write the bond pairs on the reverse of the sheet in their corresponding colours, pretending that this would be what they would look like through the spectacles. (Aiding visual memory.)

© Number Bonds Fun LDA

Activity 64 Mittens on strings

This activity reinforces the idea that the number bond pairs are commutative. Children copy the bond pairs from one mitten to its partner, changing the order of the bond as they do so.

Activity 65 Apple number search

Children find the number 20 bond pairs hidden in the apple. They are given the bond pairs at the foot of the page as an aid.

Activity 66 Hide and seek

Cut out the rectangle. The numbers in the centre, when added vertically, total 20. Cut along each dotted line, allowing you to fold the top and bottom squares over to hide the numbers. This will allow the children to test each other by hiding one or other of the bond partners for their friend to guess.

Activity 67 Bananas

Children to be given 20 counters or interlocking cubes. Children partition these counters into two subsets and record the numbers made in the banana pair. How many different number 20 bonds can they make?

Activity 68 Submarines

Children colour match the submarines with their partners to make number 50 bond pairs.

Activity 69 T-Shirt matching

Children cut out the t-shirt halves and paste them together by matching the number 50 bond pairs.

Activity 70 Fifty flowers

Children practise counting in tens. Each flower petal is worth 10 and each flower should have petals totalling 50. Can the children use their number 50 bond knowledge, or, existing petals to calculate and draw in those that are missing? Write the missing number in the centre of the flower.

Activity 71 Anchors away

Children follow the lines from the ships to the anchors to find the number 100 bond pairs. Children colour the anchor and ship pairs the same colour and then write the bond pairs on the reverse sheet.

Activity 72 Cannons and cannonballs

Children colour match the cannons with its cannonball partner to make number 100 bond pairs.

Activity 73 Number bond snakes

Children are given one of the number 100 bond partners. Children write the missing number 100 bond partner in the right-hand snake.

Activity 74 Space alien

Children cut out each rectangle containing part of the alien. They then reassemble the alien in its proper order by using their number 100 bonds.

Activity 75 Number bond crackers

Children cut out the cracker halves and paste the crackers together by matching number 100 bond pairs.

Activity 76 Number bond rockets
(Two sheets—rockets and planets)

Photocopy, decorate and laminate each sheet. Cut out the rockets. The children then match each rocket to its planet using their knowledge of the number 100 bond pairs. How quickly can they do this?

Activity 77 Racing car lotto (mixed bonds to 20)
(Two sheets—cars and winners badges)

Photocopy, decorate and laminate each sheet. Cut out the badges. The children then match each badge to its car using their knowledge of number bond pairs. How quickly can they do this?

Activity 78 Number bond addition square

Children calculate the total of the horizontal and vertical digits to map number bond pairs to 20.

Activity 79 Number bond lorries

Children write number bond pairs on the door of each lorry. The bonds they write are dictated by the number of the lorry.

Activity 80 Journey to the bottom of the sea

The game track contains number bond pairs to 10. How quickly can the children calculate these bond pairs and get to the finish?

Activity 81 Journey to the bottom of the sea

This answer sheet is provided for Activity 80 'Journey to the bottom of the sea.' This will allow the children to complete the activity with a partner who can check their answers as they go. Alternatively, Activity 81 can be used for further development by asking the children to work their way along the track giving a number bond pair for the given total.

Activity 82 Journey into space

The game track contains number bond pairs to 20. How quickly can the children calculate these bond pairs and get to the finish?

Activity 83 Journey into space (Answer sheet)

An answer sheet is provided so that the children can play with a partner independently. The partner checks the totals as they go. This sheet can also be used for further development by asking the children to work their way along the track giving a number bond pair for the given total.

© Number Bonds Fun LDA

Individual Education Plan targets

In order to support children with special educational needs in numeracy, sample IEP statements have been given below. Assessments should be made against the statements for number bond knowledge. Two or three statements should be used for the IEP and written in light of assessments made.

- Child to be able to partition a number into two sub-sets.
- Child to be able to combine two sub-sets.
- Child to be able to count reliably a set of objects to 10/20.
- Child to be able to complete a simple addition calculation.
- Child to be able to complete a simple subtraction calculation.
- Child to know number 10/20 bond pairs.
- Child to recall number facts to 10/20.
- Child to recognise two numbers that when combined total . . . .
- Child to give two numbers with a total of . . . .
- Child to recognise the relationship between two numbers.
- Child to predict a simple pattern in partitioning and combining numbers.
- Child to identify missing bond partner given total and one of the bond partners.

Notes

- These number bond activity sheets are intended as a support material and not as a substitute for practical work. Opportunities for practical exploration of partitioning and combining numbers should be taken.

- These sheets can be used as part of the daily numeracy lessons, either by enlarging and using as a whole class Oral Work-Mental Starter/Plenary or as an individual or group activity.

- The children should be encouraged to look for patterns in partitioning and combining. For this reason, the authors have included number bonds for 50 and 100 in multiples of ten so that the connection can be made between bonds for 5/50 and 10/100.

- 'Find the bond pairs by following lines' activity sheets have been included as an introductory activity for those number bonds which the children may not have encountered before.

- These activities could also be used as a basis for a display in the classroom.

Name _____

Activity 1
Number 5 bonds

Follow the mice to find the bonds for number 5.

© Number Bonds Fun LDA

10

Name_____

Activity 2
Number 5 bonds

Practise your bonds for number 5.

© Number Bonds Fun LDA

Name_____

Activity 3
Number 5 bonds

Colour match the buckets and spades to make your number bonds to five.

Activity 4
Number 5 bonds

Name _____

Look at the number at the bottom of each tower and colour that many blocks.
Write how many blocks are not coloured in the box at the top of the tower.

0   1   2   3   4   5

© Number Bonds Fun LDA

Name _____

Activity 5
Number 5 bonds

Colour the dice pair that score 5 in blue, the others in green.

Name_____

Activity 6
Number 6 bonds

Follow the dogs' leads to find the bonds for number 6.
Colour match the dog to its lead.

© Number Bonds Fun LDA

Name_____

Activity 7
Number 6 bonds

Practise your bonds for number 6.
Help the caterpillars to cross the leaves.

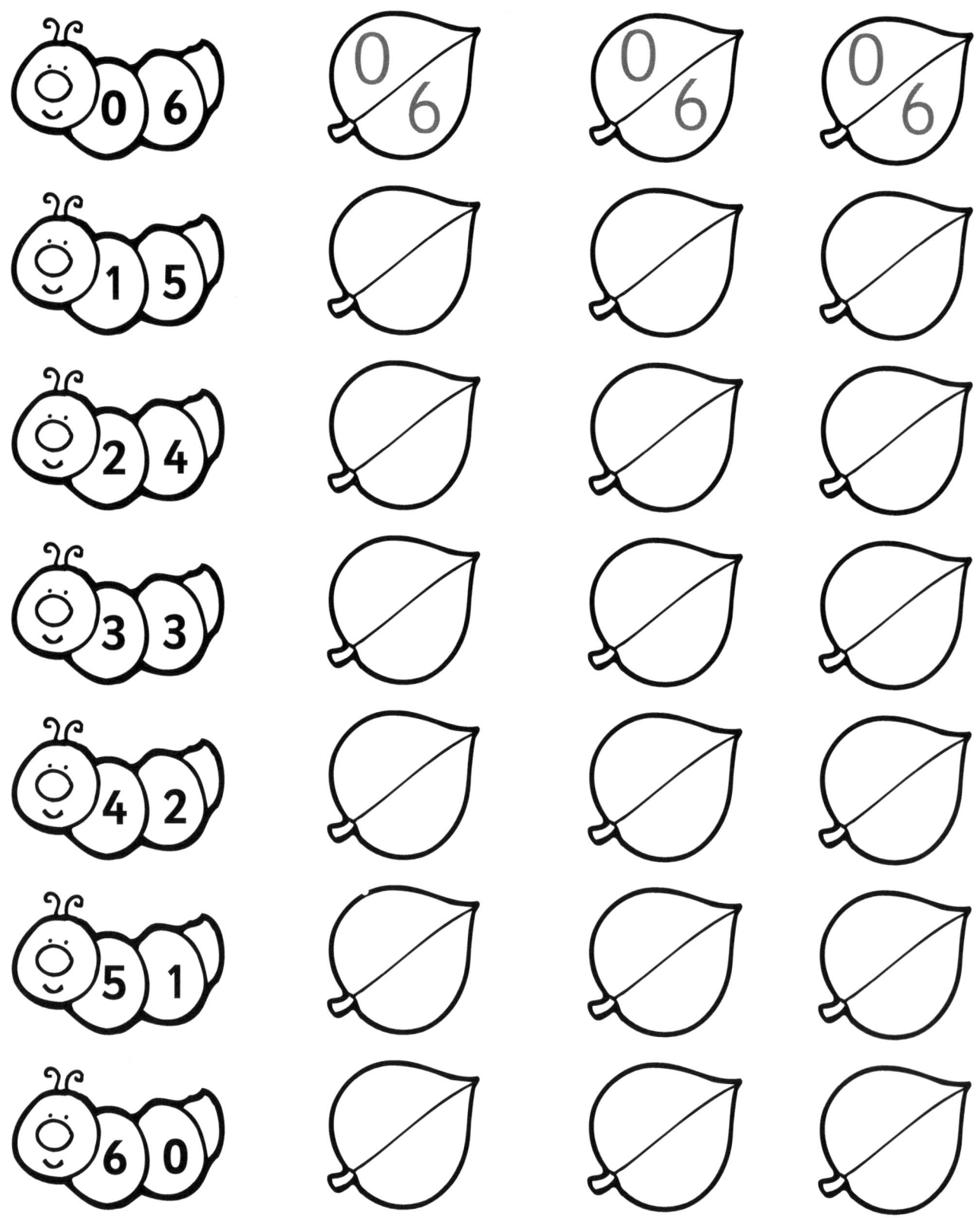

Colour each bond pair a different colour and always look for number patterns.

© Number Bonds Fun LDA

Name_____

Activity 8
Number 6 bonds

Colour match the crabs with the shells to make 6.

17

Activity 9
Number 6 bonds

Name

Use two colours to show the two numbers that make 6.

© Number Bonds Fun LDA

Name_____

Activity 10
Number 6 bonds

Count the socks and hankies on each line to help you learn your bonds for number 6.

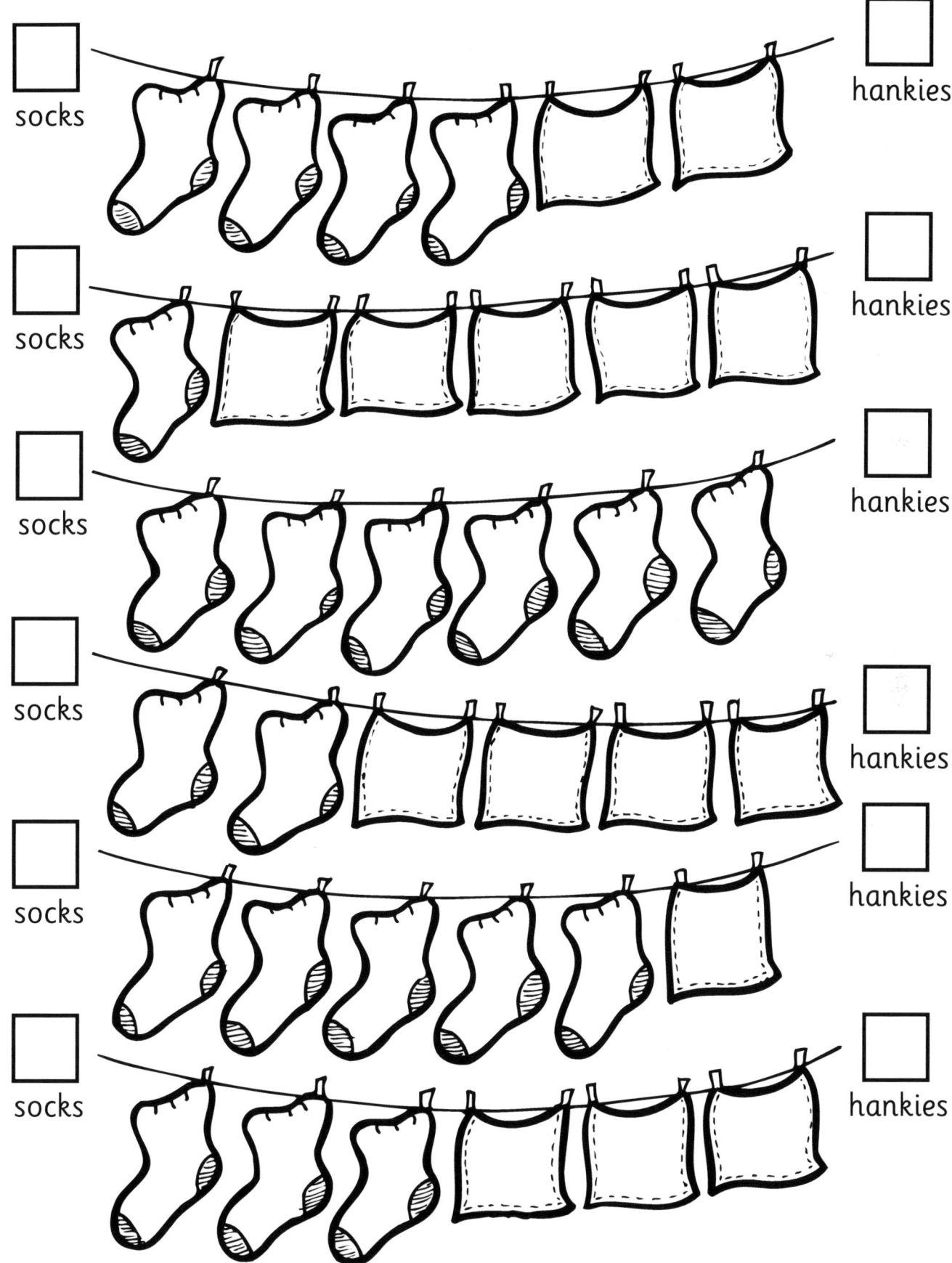

Name _____ Activity 11
Number 7 bonds

Follow the balloon trails to find the bonds for number 7.

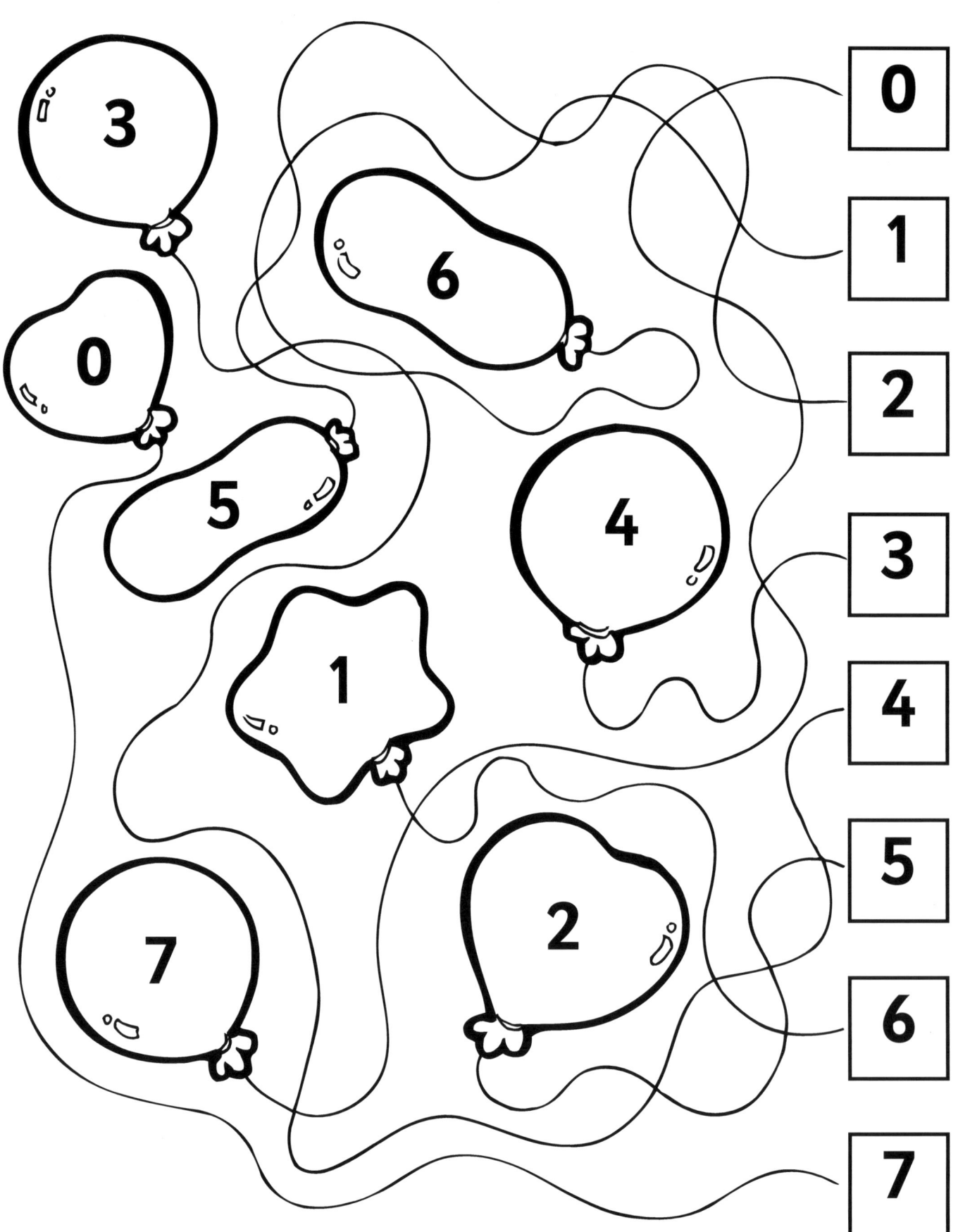

Colour the balloon and the box the same colour.

Name_____ Activity 12
Number 7 bonds

Practise your bonds for number 7.

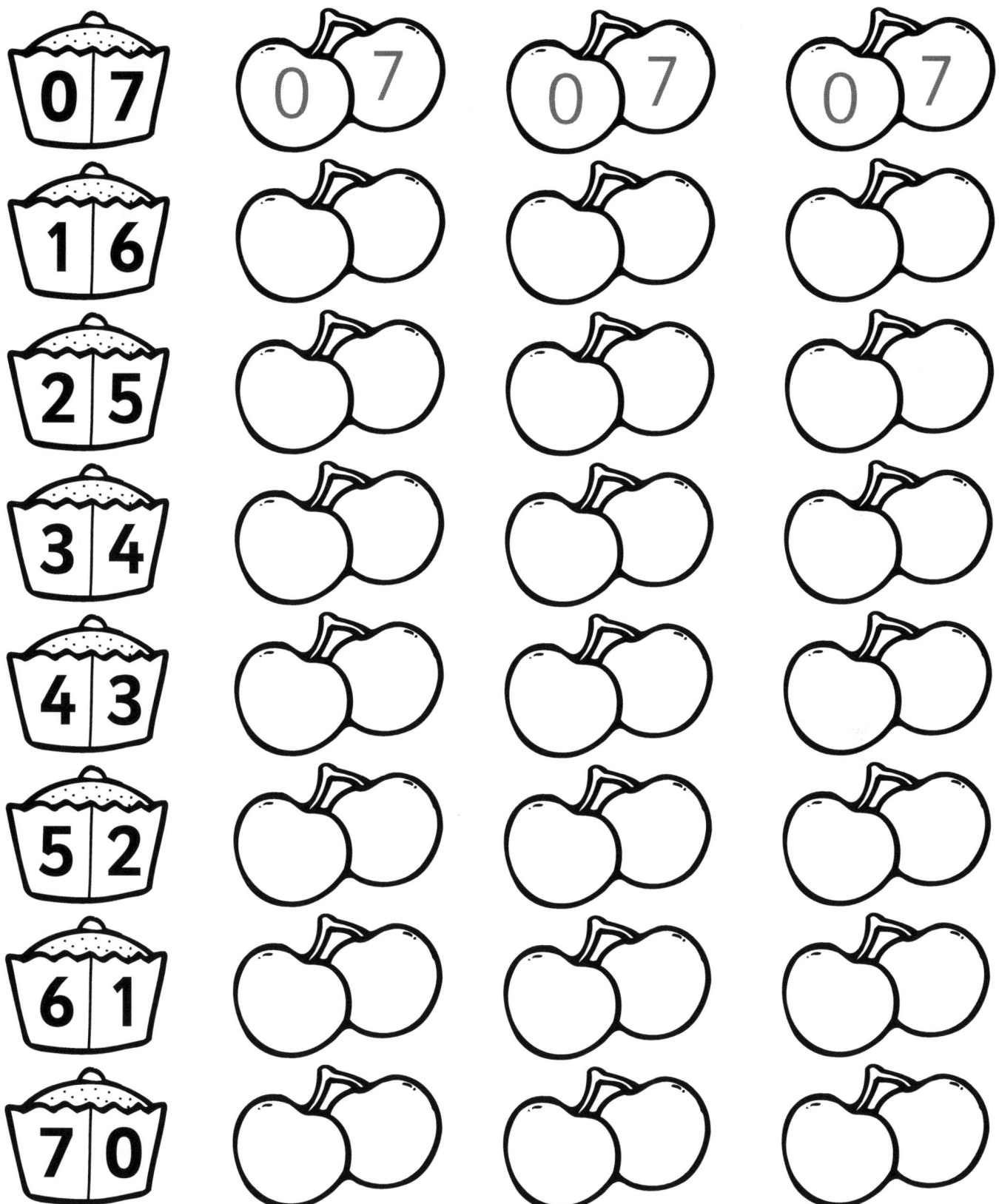

Colour each bond pair a different colour and always look for patterns.

Name_____

Activity 13
Number 7 bonds

Colour match the bows and arrows to make number bonds for seven.

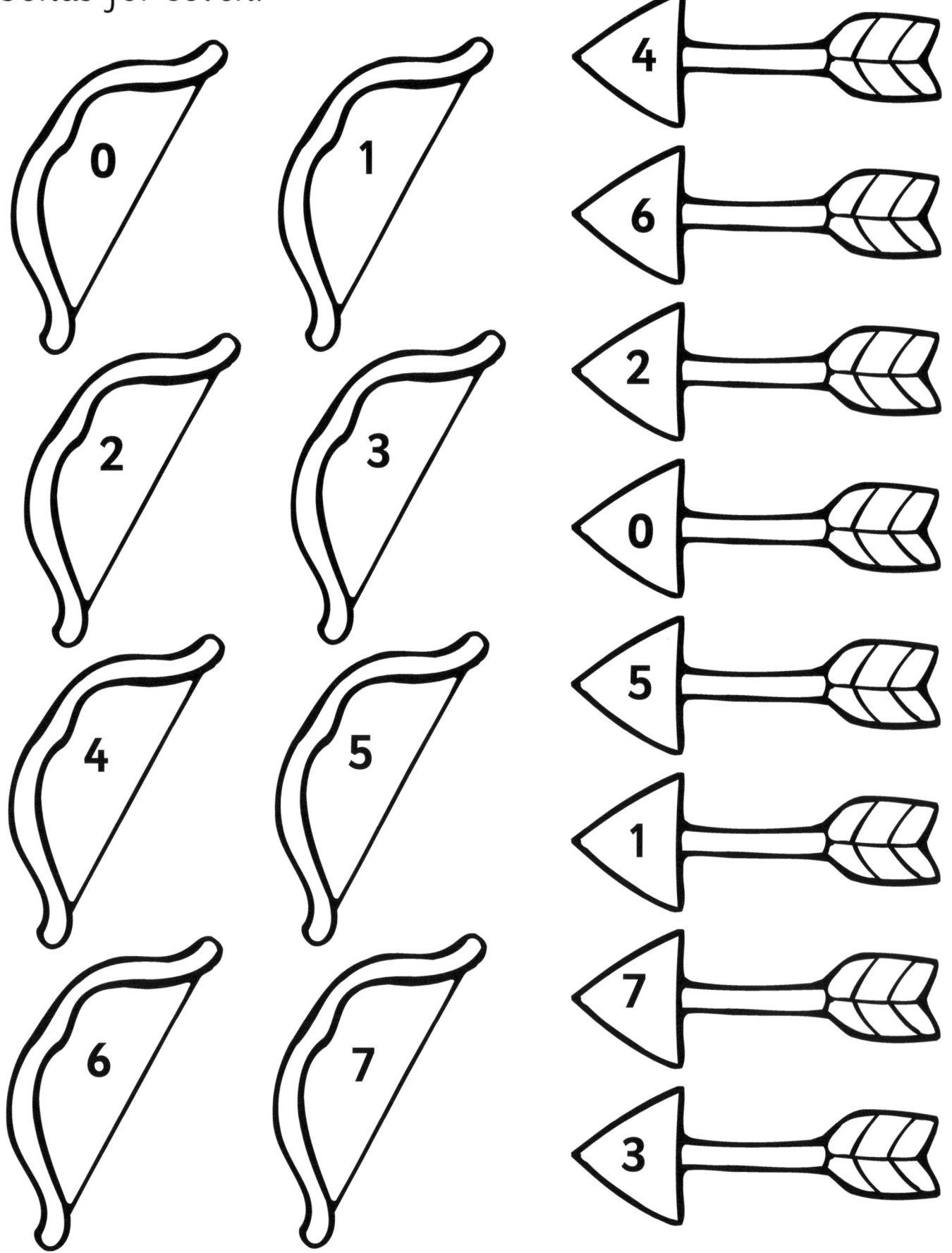

© Number Bonds Fun LDA

Name_____

Activity 14
Number 7 bonds

Can you find the sailing boats that are in the number 7 race?

Colour the boats that total 7 yellow.
Colour all other boats red.

© Number Bonds Fun LDA

Name _____ Activity 15
Number 7 bonds

Each crown has 7 jewels. Use two colours and your number 7 bonds to colour the jewels.

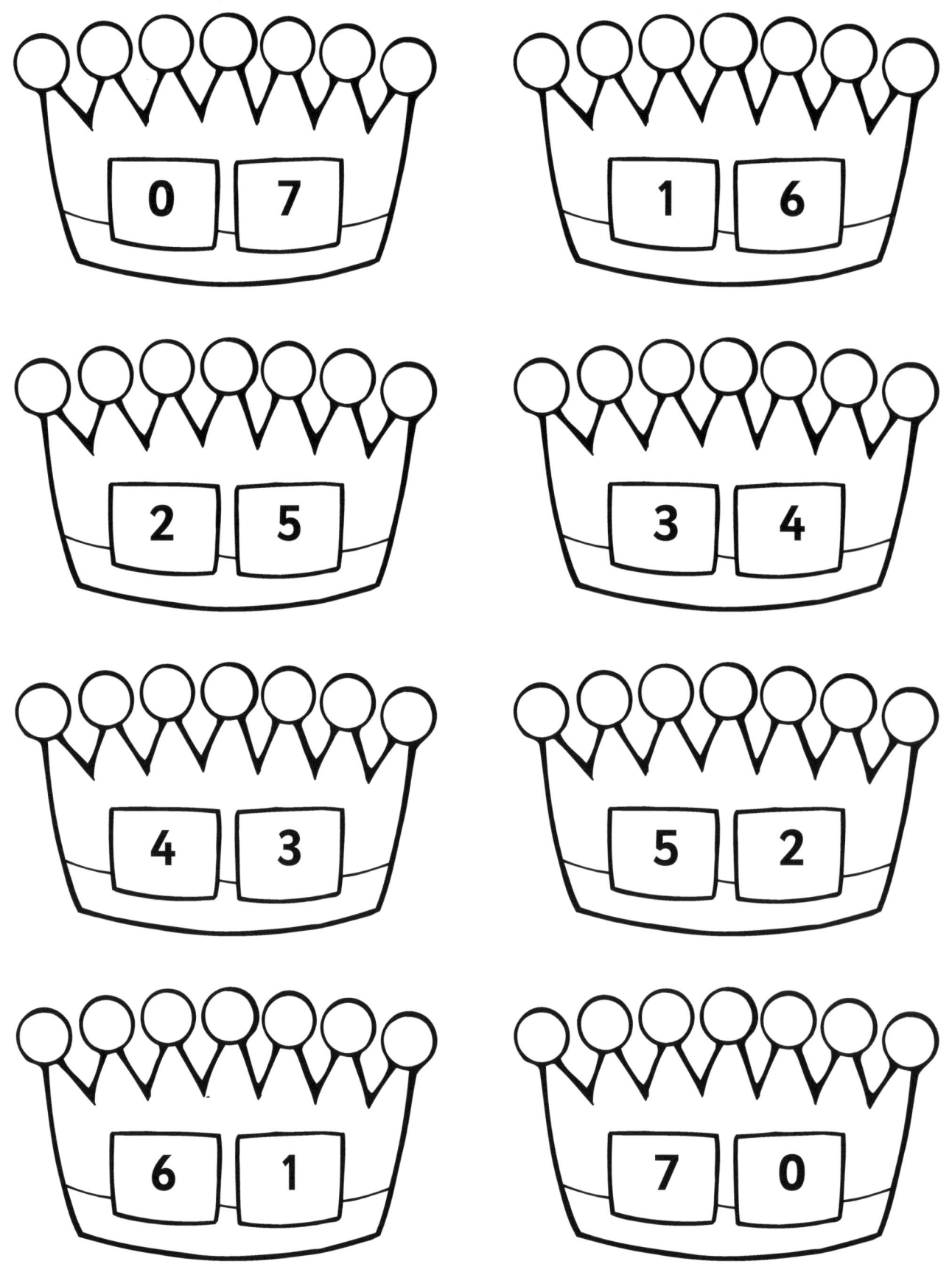

Name _____ Activity 16
Number 8 bonds

Follow the yo-yo strings to find the bonds for number 8.

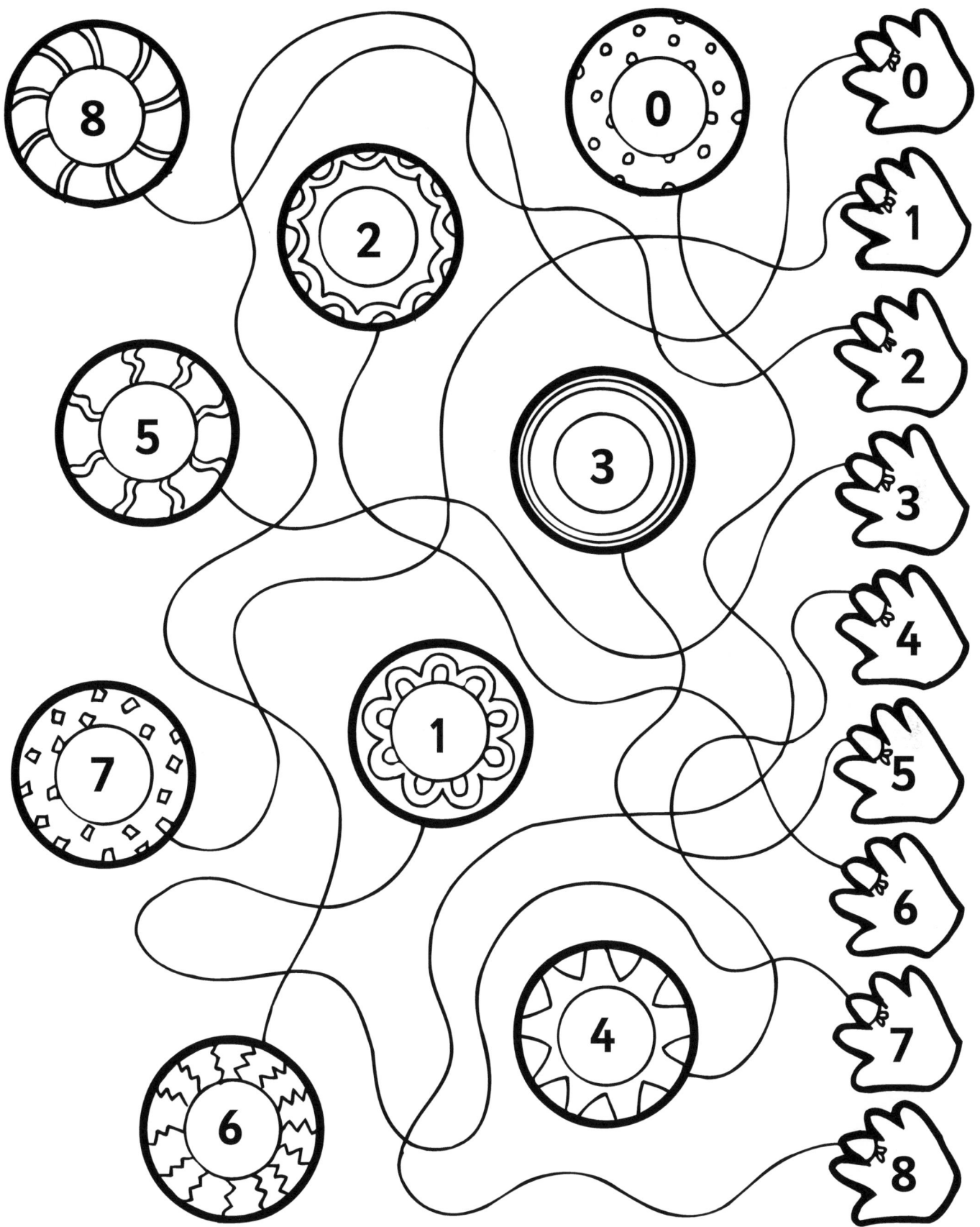

Colour the yo-yos and hands the same colour.

© Number Bonds Fun LDA

Name _____

Activity 17
Number 8 bonds

Practise your bonds for number 8.

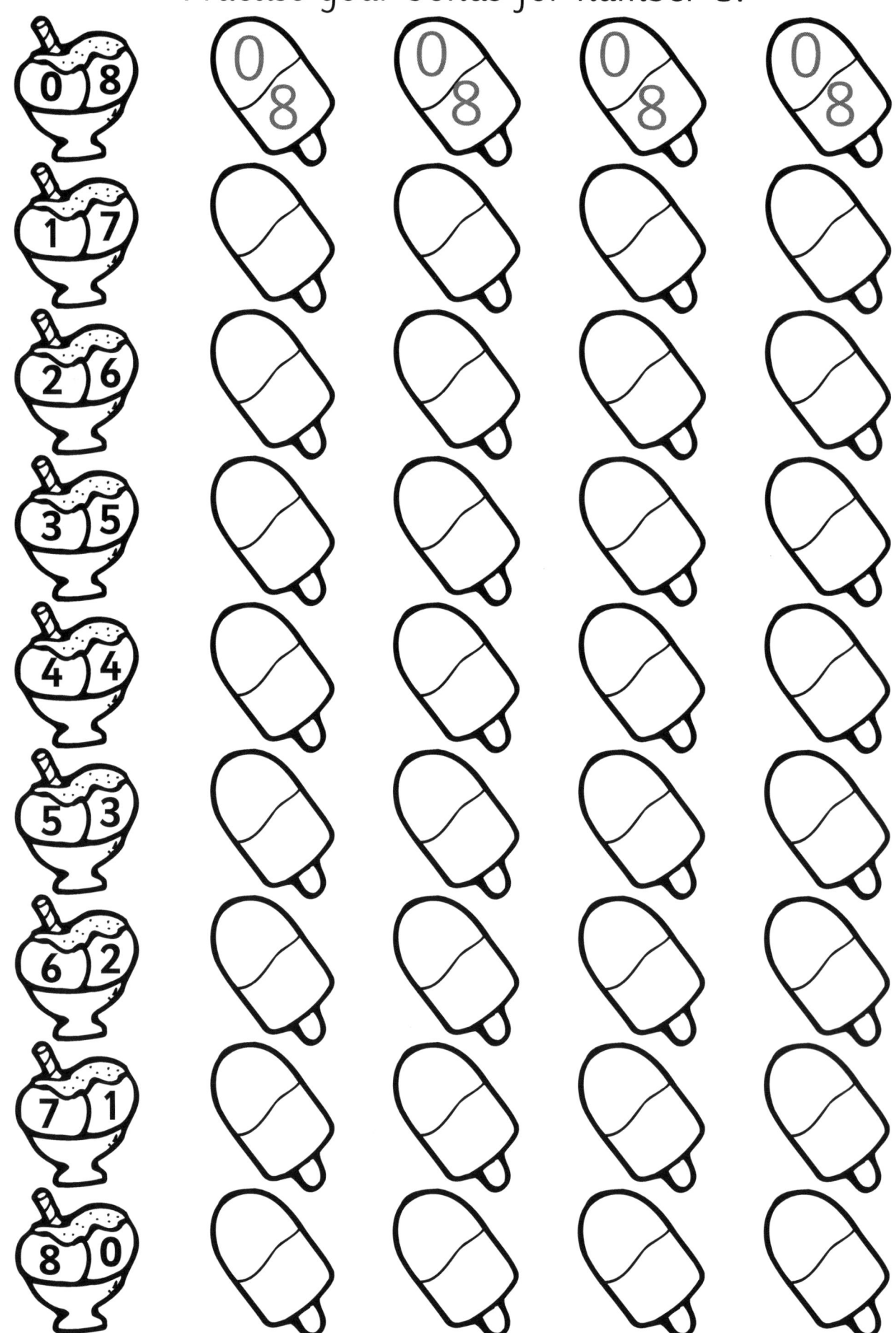

© Number Bonds Fun LDA

Name _____

Activity 18
Number 8 bonds

Use your number 8 bonds to work out which key opens each door. Match the pairs using the same colour.

© Number Bonds Fun LDA

Name _____

Activity 19
Number 8 bonds

Each flag has 8 pieces. Choose two colours and colour the flags to show the number bond pairs.

Name _____

Activity 20
Number 8 bonds

Domino Colouring

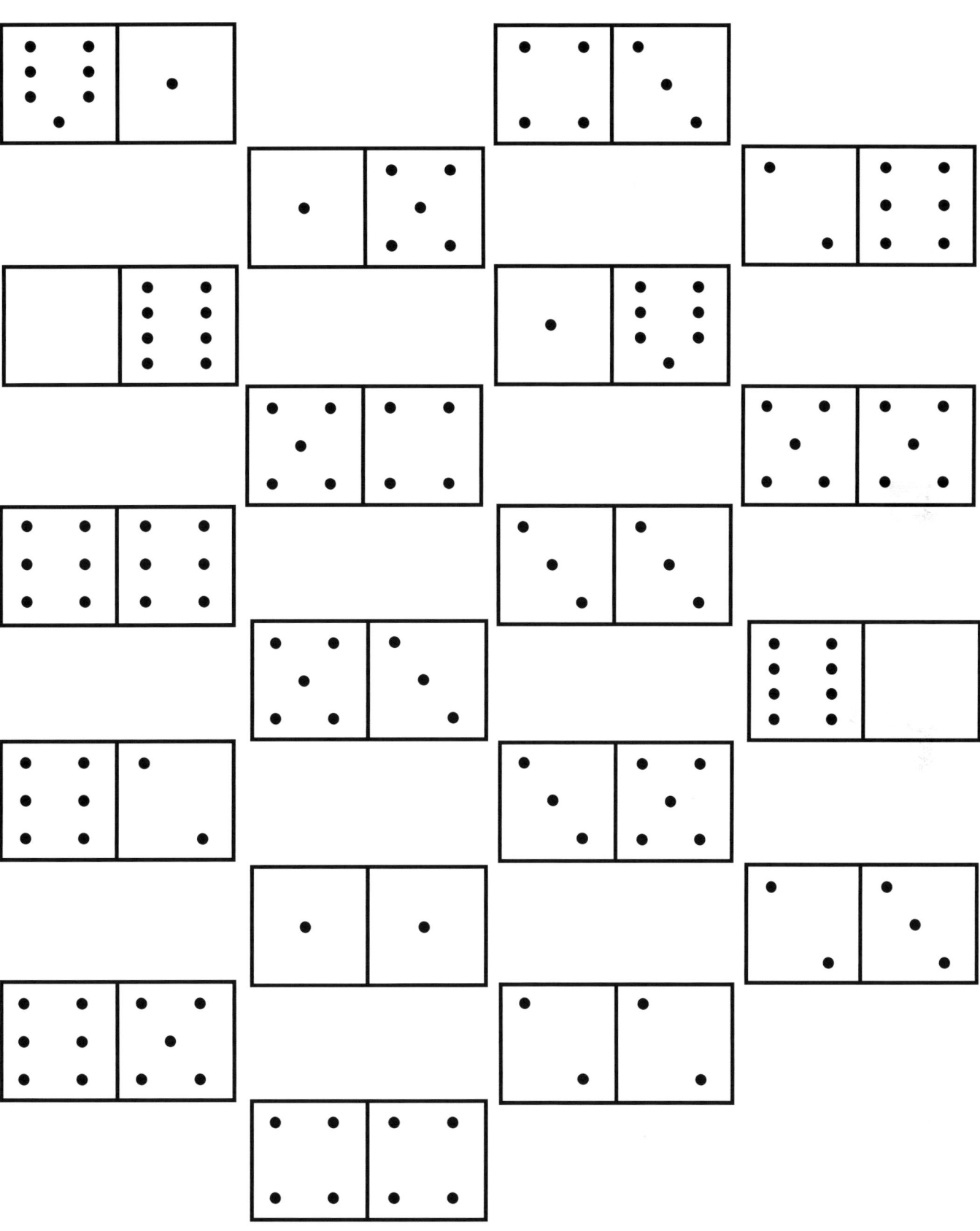

Colour dominoes worth 8 red.
Colour other dominoes green.

© Number Bonds Fun LDA

Name _____

Activity 21
Number 9 bonds

Follow the kite strings to find the bonds for number 9.

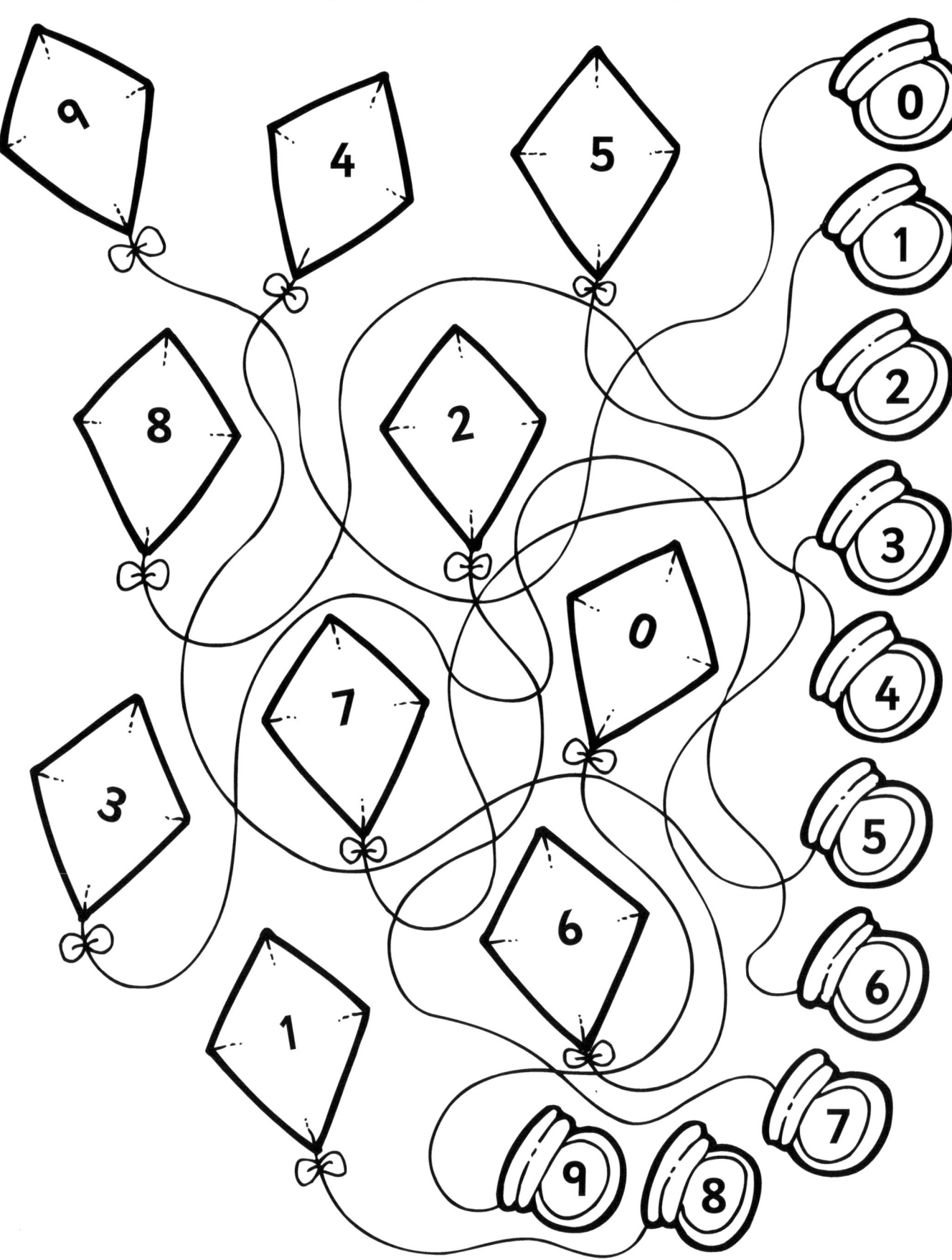

Colour the kite and handle pairs the same.

Name _____

Activity 22
Number 9 bonds

Practise your number bonds to 9.
Use a different colour for each pair.

0 9
1 8
2 7
3 6
4 5
5 4
6 3
7 2
8 1
9 0

© Number Bonds Fun LDA

Name _____

Activity 23
Number 9 bonds

Colour match the shampoo bottles and the bubbles to make 9.

Name _____   Activity 24
                                 Number 9 bonds

Each necklace has 9 pieces. Choose two colours and colour the necklaces to show the number 9 bond pairs.

Name _____

Activity 25
Number 9 bonds

Which suitcases belong to aeroplane number 9?

Colour suitcases worth 9 orange and all others blue.

Name _____

Activity 26
Number 10 bonds

Follow the spaghetti to find the bonds for 10.
Colour match the meatball with the right fork.

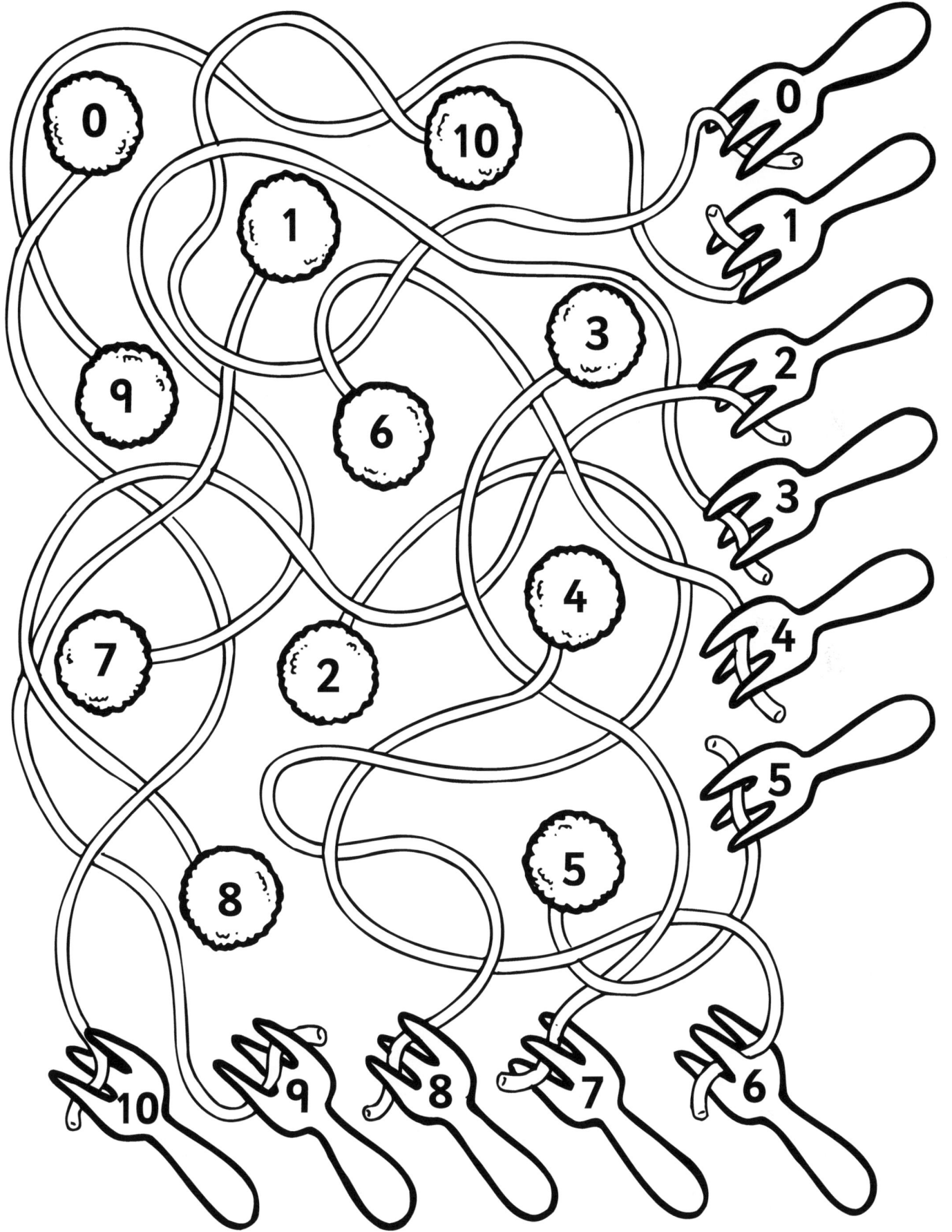

© Number Bonds Fun LDA   35

Activity 27
Number 10 bonds

Name _____

Practise your bonds for number 10 and colour each pair a different colour.

5 / 5
6 / 4
7 / 3
8 / 2
9 / 1
10 / 0

0 / 10
1 / 9
2 / 8
3 / 7
4 / 6

© Number Bonds Fun LDA
36

Name _____

Activity 28
Number 10 bonds

There are 22 balloons floating in the sky. Can you colour the balloons to make bonds for number 10?

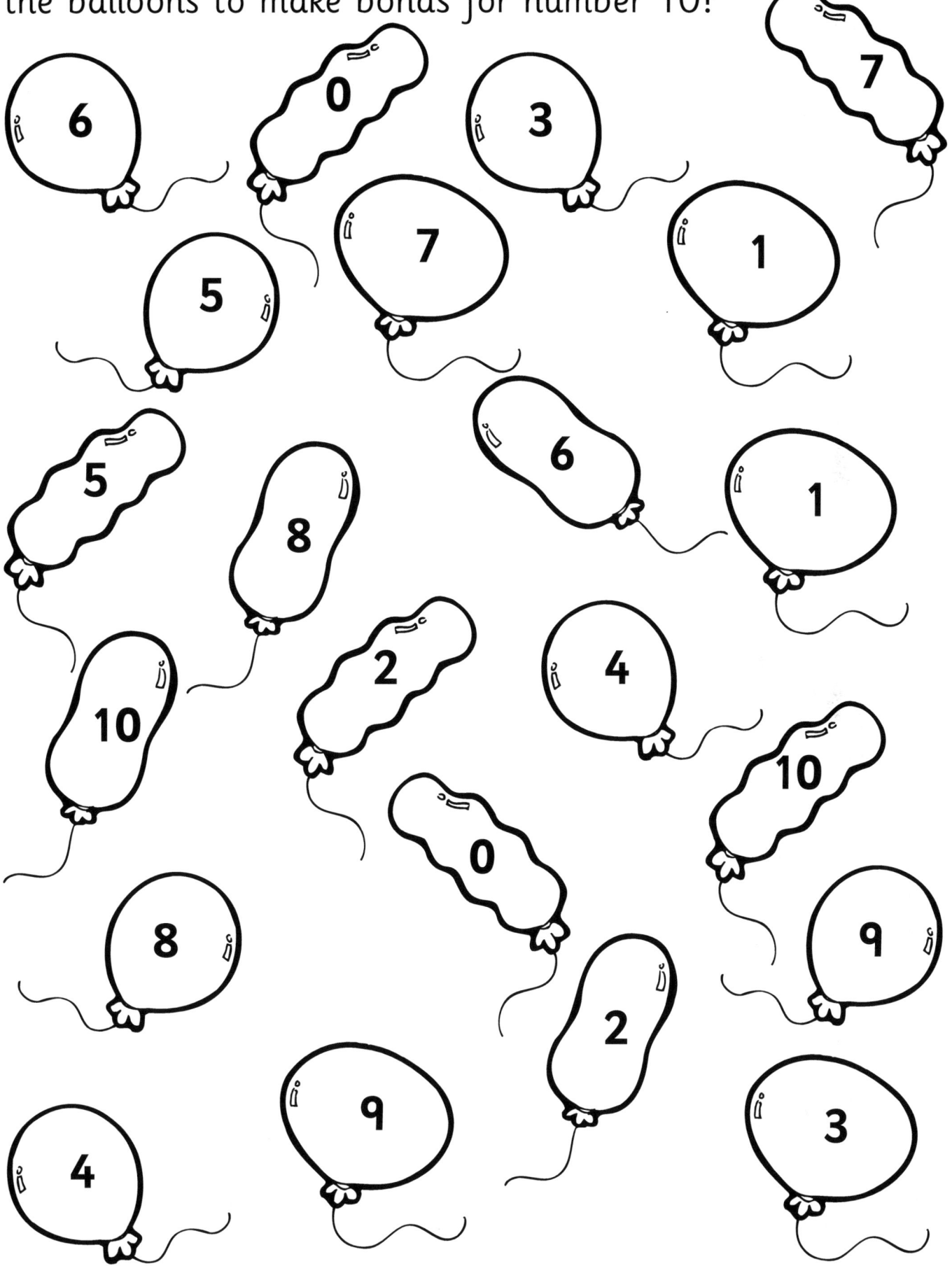

6, 0, 3, 7, 5, 7, 1, 5, 8, 6, 1, 10, 2, 4, 0, 10, 8, 9, 2, 4, 9, 3

© Number Bonds Fun LDA

37

Name _____

Activity 29
Number 10 bonds

Number bond memory rhyme

0 and 10 two fat men.
1 and 9 all is fine.
2 and 8 at the gate.
3 and 7 gone to Devon.
4 and 6 funny tricks.
5 and 5 swim and dive.
6 and 4 knock at the door.
7 and 3 cup of tea.
8 and 2 a pot of stew.
9 and 1 nearly gone.
10 and 0 always a hero.

Copy, write and learn this rhyme.

Choose two number bond pairs from the rhyme and draw a picture of each.

© Number Bonds Fun LDA

Name _____

Activity 30
Number 10 bonds

Can you find the number bond pairs hiding next to each other in this necklace? Colour the pairs when you find them.

© Number Bonds Fun LDA

39

Name _____

Activity 31
Number 10 bonds

Each tree had 10 apples. How many should be left on each tree? Draw them on.

© Number Bonds Fun LDA

Name _____

Activity 32
Number 10 bonds

Can you find the hidden object? Colour only the shapes with sums that add up to 10.

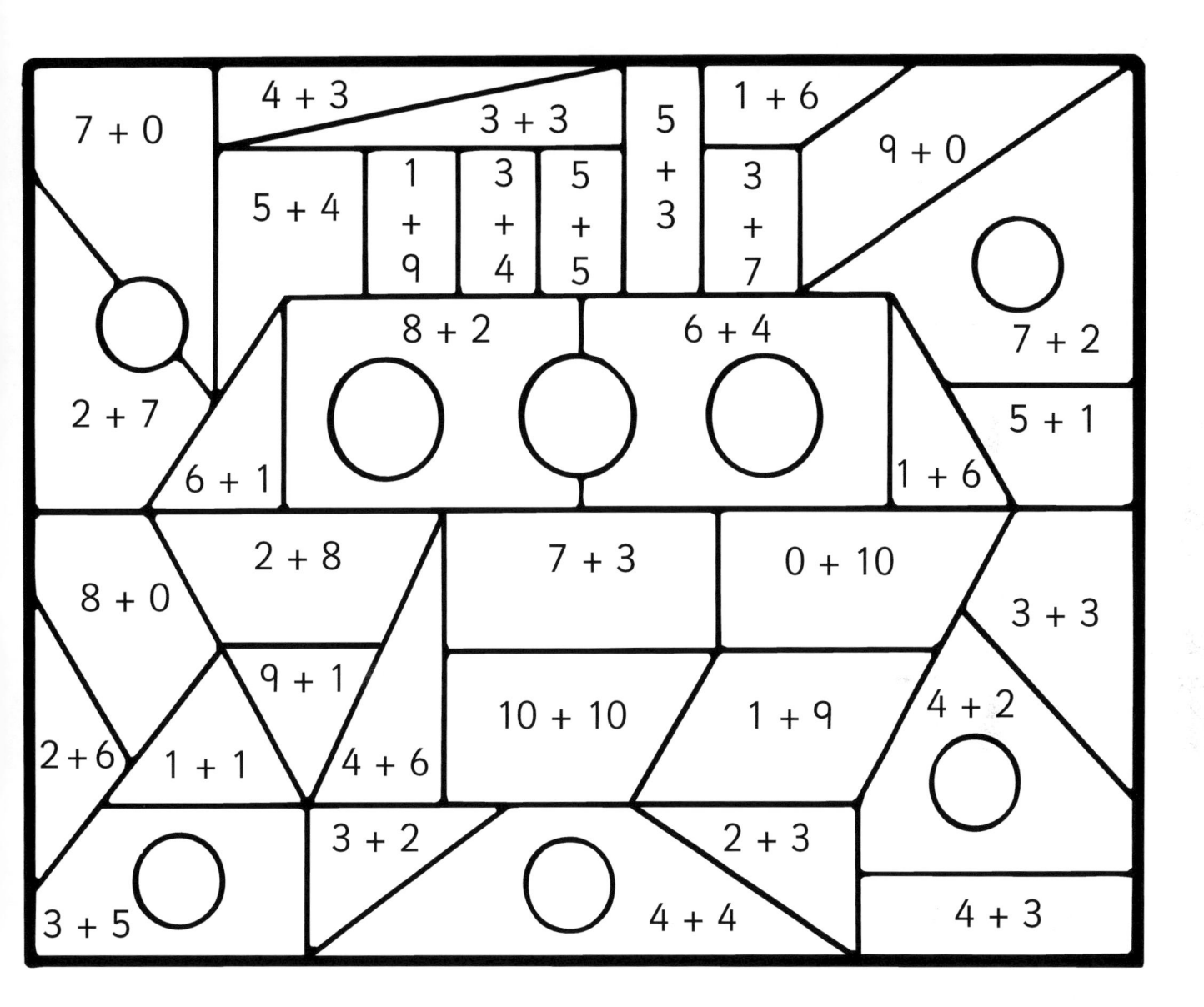

7 + 0	4 + 3		3 + 3		5 + 3		1 + 6	9 + 0	
	5 + 4	1 + 9	3 + 4	5 + 5		3 + 7			
		8 + 2		6 + 4			7 + 2
2 + 7						5 + 1
	6 + 1				1 + 6	
8 + 0	2 + 8	7 + 3	0 + 10	3 + 3
	9 + 1			
2 + 6	1 + 1	4 + 6	10 + 10	1 + 9	4 + 2
3 + 5	3 + 2	4 + 4	2 + 3	4 + 3

Write all of the sums that do not add up to 10 below.

Name _____

Activity 33
Number 10 bonds

Can you find the hidden object? Colour only the shapes with sums that add up to 10.

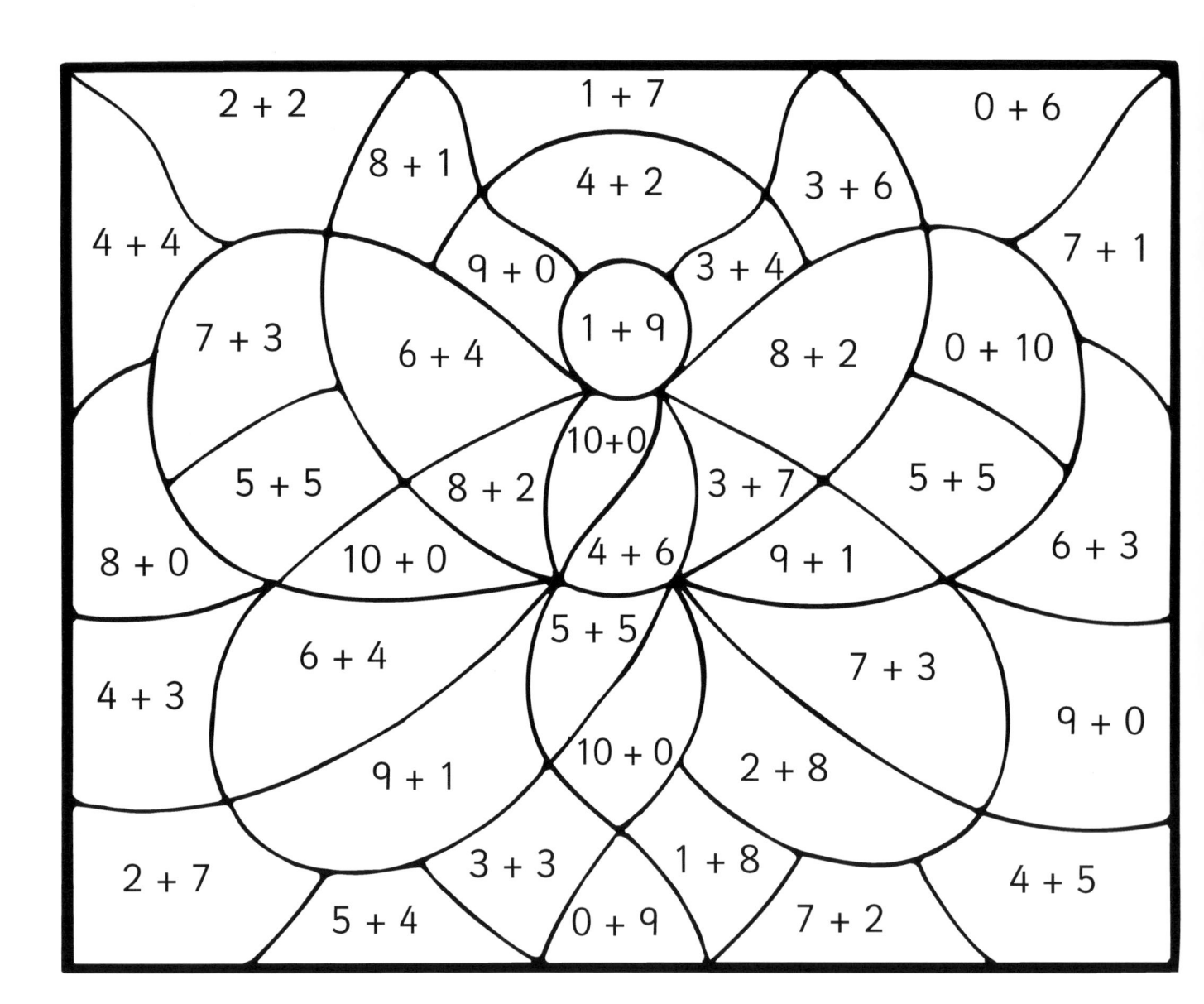

2 + 2	1 + 7		0 + 6
8 + 1	4 + 2	3 + 6	
4 + 4	9 + 0	3 + 4	7 + 1
7 + 3	6 + 4	1 + 9	8 + 2	0 + 10
		10 + 0		
5 + 5	8 + 2	3 + 7	5 + 5
8 + 0	10 + 0	4 + 6	9 + 1	6 + 3
		5 + 5		
4 + 3	6 + 4		7 + 3	9 + 0
	9 + 1	10 + 0	2 + 8	
2 + 7	3 + 3	1 + 8	4 + 5
	5 + 4	0 + 9	7 + 2	

Write all the sums that do not add up to 10 below.

© Number Bonds Fun LDA

Name _____

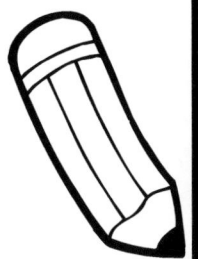

Activity 34
Number 10 bonds

1	5	2	4	6	9	3	0
5	2	3	5	8	1	4	10
3	4	2	1	6	3	9	5
10	0	7	9	5	8	6	10
5	6	10	3	9	2	4	9
3	7	5	6	4	5	10	7
9	10	4	1	3	10	8	3
2	8	5	10	5	5	4	3

Can you find number bond pairs that make 10? The pairs must must lie horizontally, vertically or diagonally.

10 + 0   5 + 5
9 + 1   4 + 6
8 + 2   3 + 7
7 + 3   2 + 8
6 + 4   1 + 9
     0 + 10

© Number Bonds Fun LDA

Name _____

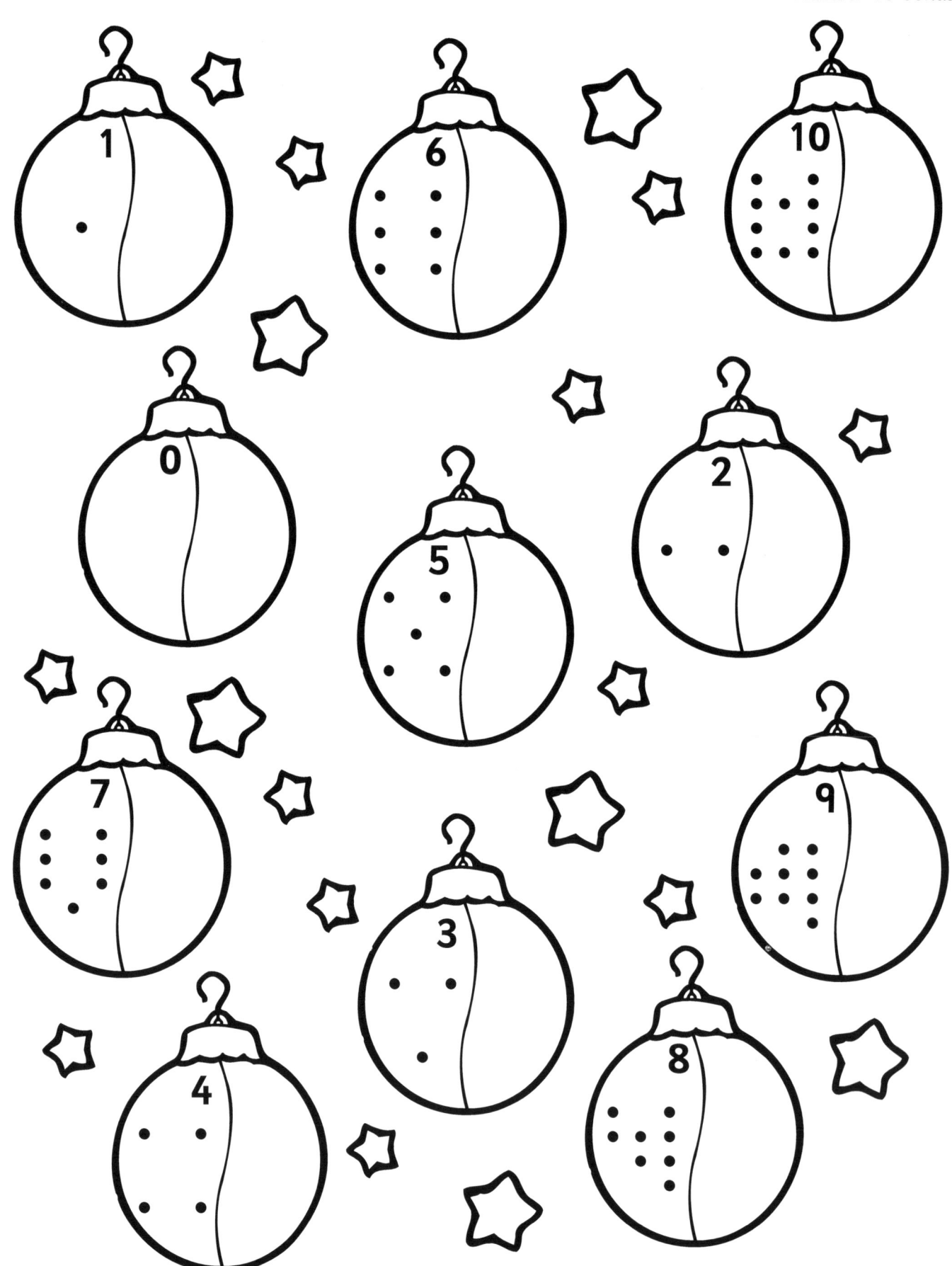

Activity 35
Number 10 bonds

Draw the missing number of spots to make 10 on each bauble.

© Number Bonds Fun LDA

Name _____

Activity 36
Number 10 bonds

Each ladybird needs a total of 10 spots. Draw the missing spots on the right-hand side of each ladybird.

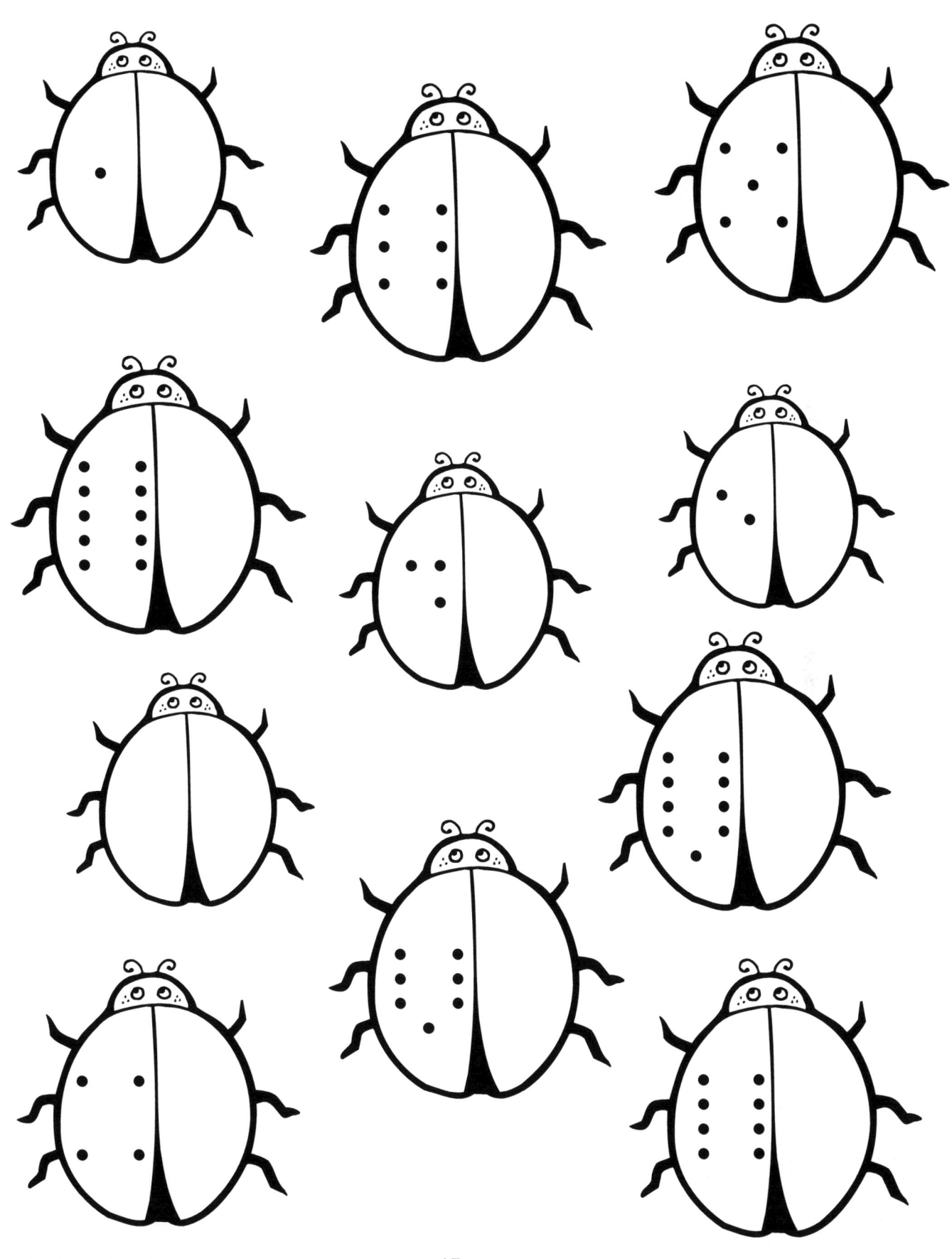

45

© Number Bonds Fun LDA

Name _____

Activity 37
Number 10 bonds

Use your fingers to help you with number bonds to 10. Count how many fingers are up and how many fingers are down.

1	ups and	9	downs
☐	ups and	☐	downs
☐	ups and	☐	downs
☐	ups and	☐	downs
☐	ups and	☐	downs
☐	ups and	☐	downs
☐	ups and	☐	downs
☐	ups and	☐	downs
☐	ups and	☐	downs
☐	ups and	☐	downs
☐	ups and	☐	downs

© Number Bonds Fun LDA

Activity 38
Number 10 bonds

0	1	2	3	4	5
6	7	8	9	10	★ J 6 7 8 9 10 ★ O K E R 1 2 3 4 5

Photocopy this activity sheet twice to make a set of "Number Bond Pairs" or "Number Bond Snap" cards. Joker cards can be used as any number for a number bond.

© Number Bonds Fun LDA 47

Name _____

Activity 38
Number 10 bonds

Playing cards for number 10 bond pairs

10	9	8	7
0	1	2	3
6	5	4	3
4	5	6	7
	2	1	0
	8	9	10

© Number Bonds Fun LDA

Name _____

Activity 39
Number 10 bonds

Use your number bonds to help you make a curved ruler drawing. Join a number on the vertical axis to its bond pair on the horizontal axis.

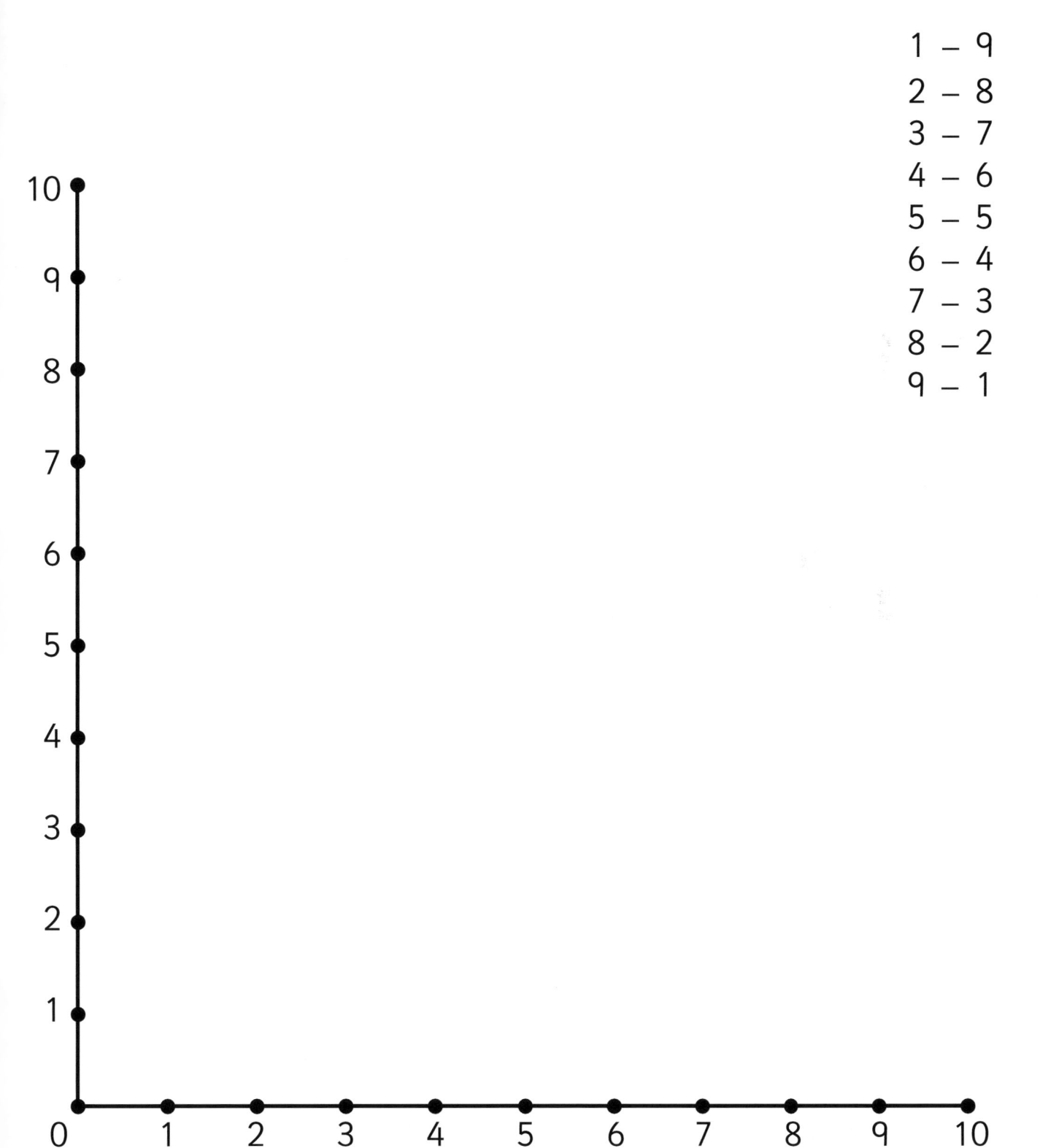

1 – 9
2 – 8
3 – 7
4 – 6
5 – 5
6 – 4
7 – 3
8 – 2
9 – 1

© Number Bonds Fun LDA

Activity 40
Number 10 bonds

Name _____

Each pie has 10 slices. Choose two colours and colour the pies to show the number pairs. Can you see a pattern in the pies?

0 and 10

10 and 0

1 and 9

2 and 8

3 and 7

4 and 6

5 and 5

6 and 4

7 and 3

8 and 2

9 and 1

© Number Bonds Fun LDA

Name _____

Activity 41
Number 10 bonds

Can you crack the code? Write the answers in the boxes at the bottom of the page. Start on the left.

▲ There are 10 books on a shelf. Three fall off. How many are left?

▲ 10 children go out to play. 6 of them are girls. How many boys are there?

▲ Lucy has 10 cakes on a plate. Her friends eat 2. How many cakes are left on the plate?

▲ George has 10p. He spends 8p. How much money does he have left?

▲ John had 5 marbles. His sister Emma had 10. How many more than John did she have?

▲ A clown had 10 balloons. One went pop. How many balloons were left?

▲ 10 fish lived in a pond. 4 were spotty. How many were not spotty?

▲ A bus can carry 5 children. How many children can 2 buses carry?

▲ There were 10 bottles of milk in the kitchen. 9 were full. How many were empty?

▲ 10 flowers were growing in the garden. Mum picked 7. How many were left?

▲ 10 birds were on a wire. 10 flew away. How many were left?

What is the hidden code?

☐ ☐ ☐ ☐ ☐ ☐ ☐ ☐ ☐ ☐ ☐

© Number Bonds Fun LDA

Name _____

Activity 42
Number 11 bonds

Match the fish to the hook to make number 11.

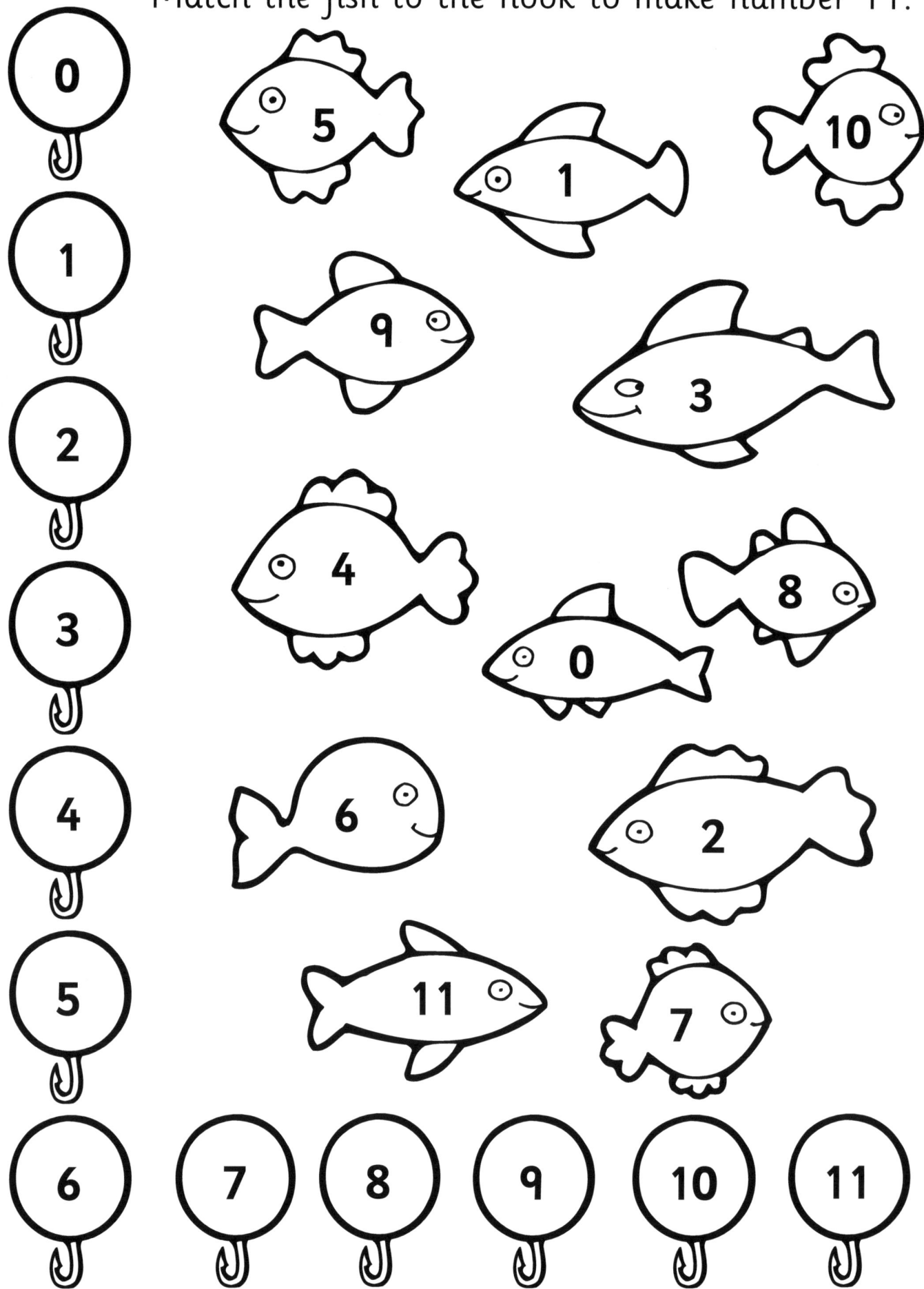

© Number Bonds Fun LDA

Activity 43
Number 11 bonds

Name _____

Cut out the magic carpets and put them in order starting with 11 and 0.

10 and 1	9 and 2	11 and 0
6 and 5	1 and 10	4 and 7
7 and 4	8 and 3	5 and 6
2 and 9	0 and 11	3 and 8

© Number Bonds Fun LDA

Name _____

Activity 44
Number 12 bonds

Find the path along the stones by colouring the missing numbers for number bonds for 12.

0 and [12]
8 and ☐
1 and ☐
7 and ☐
4 and ☐
6 and ☐
9 and ☐
3 and ☐
11 and ☐
5 and ☐
2 and ☐
12 and ☐
10 and ☐

© Number Bonds Fun LDA

Name _____

Activity 45
Number 12 bonds

Cut and stick the fish to make number bond 12 pairs.

© Number Bonds Fun LDA

Name _____

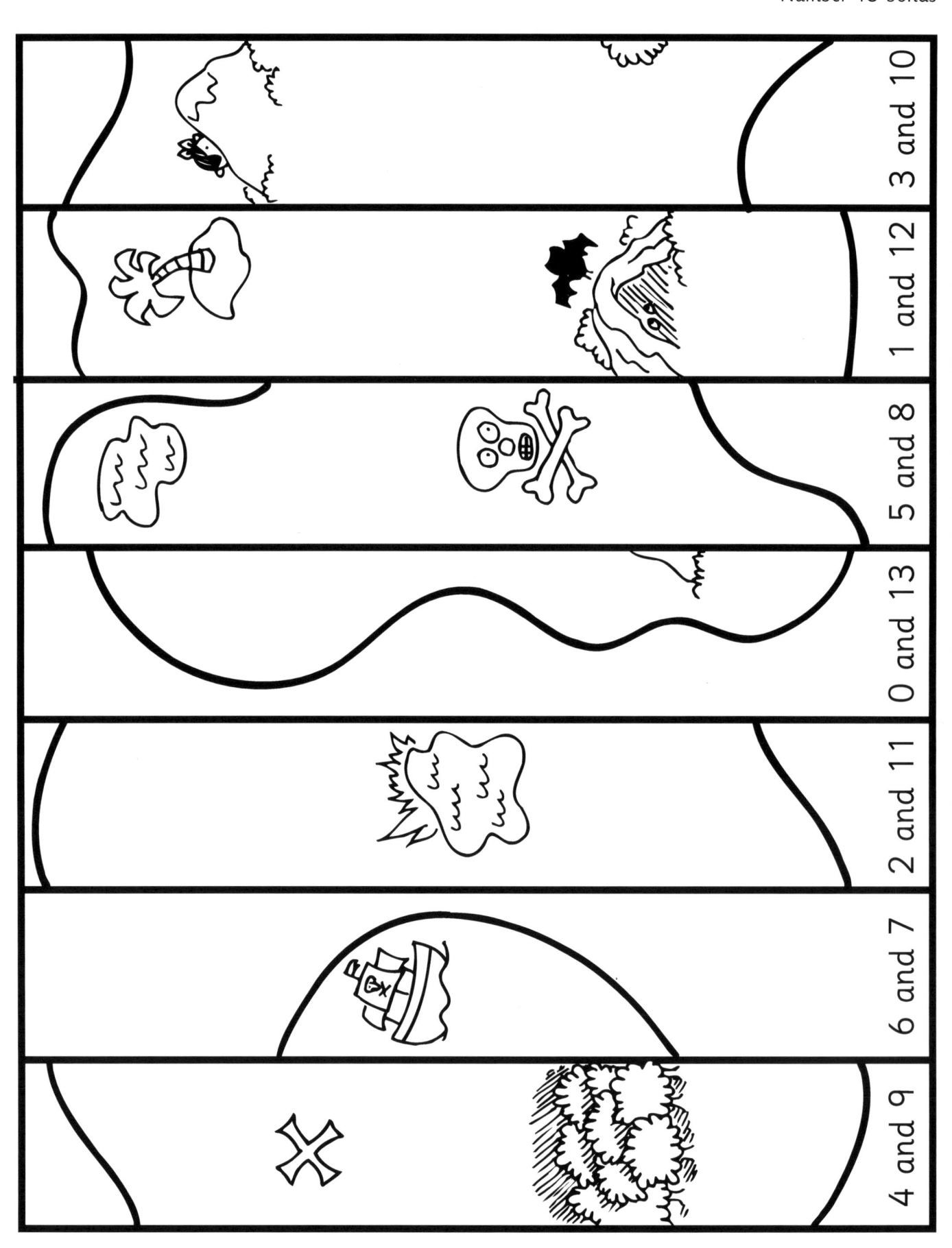

Activity 46
Number 13 bonds

3 and 10

1 and 12

5 and 8

0 and 13

2 and 11

6 and 7

4 and 9

Use your number 13 bonds to put the treasure map back together. Cut up the pieces and put them in the right order.

© Number Bonds Fun LDA
56

Name _____

Activity 47
Number 13 bonds

Can you find the number bond pairs?

Which bond pairs make 13?

ON/OFF   +

9	4	2	4	5	2	11	10
1	8	3	6	7	8	1	9
0	13	4	7	5	13	0	1
13	12	1	2	6	1	5	11
8	5	5	1	12	2	7	6
6	10	10	3	6	3	5	4
3	10	11	3	7	4	9	8
11	4	12	5	8	9	11	2

0 + 13   3 + 10   7 + 6   11 + 2
1 + 12   4 + 9   8 + 5   12 + 1
2 + 11   5 + 8   9 + 4   13 + 0
            6 + 7   10 + 3

All bond pairs lie horizontally.

© Number Bonds Fun LDA   57

Name _____

Activity 48
Number 14 bonds

How many different ways can you find to break 14 into number pairs?

Write the number bond pairs in the cherries.

© Number Bonds Fun LDA

Name _____

Activity 49
Number 14 bonds

Colour match the eggs to the nests using your number 14 bonds.

© Number Bonds Fun LDA

Name _____

Activity 50
Number 15 bonds

Each strip measures 15cm, but is divided into 2. Measure each part of the strip and write it in each box.

Name _____

Activity 51
Number 15 bonds

Can you find the number pairs to make 15?

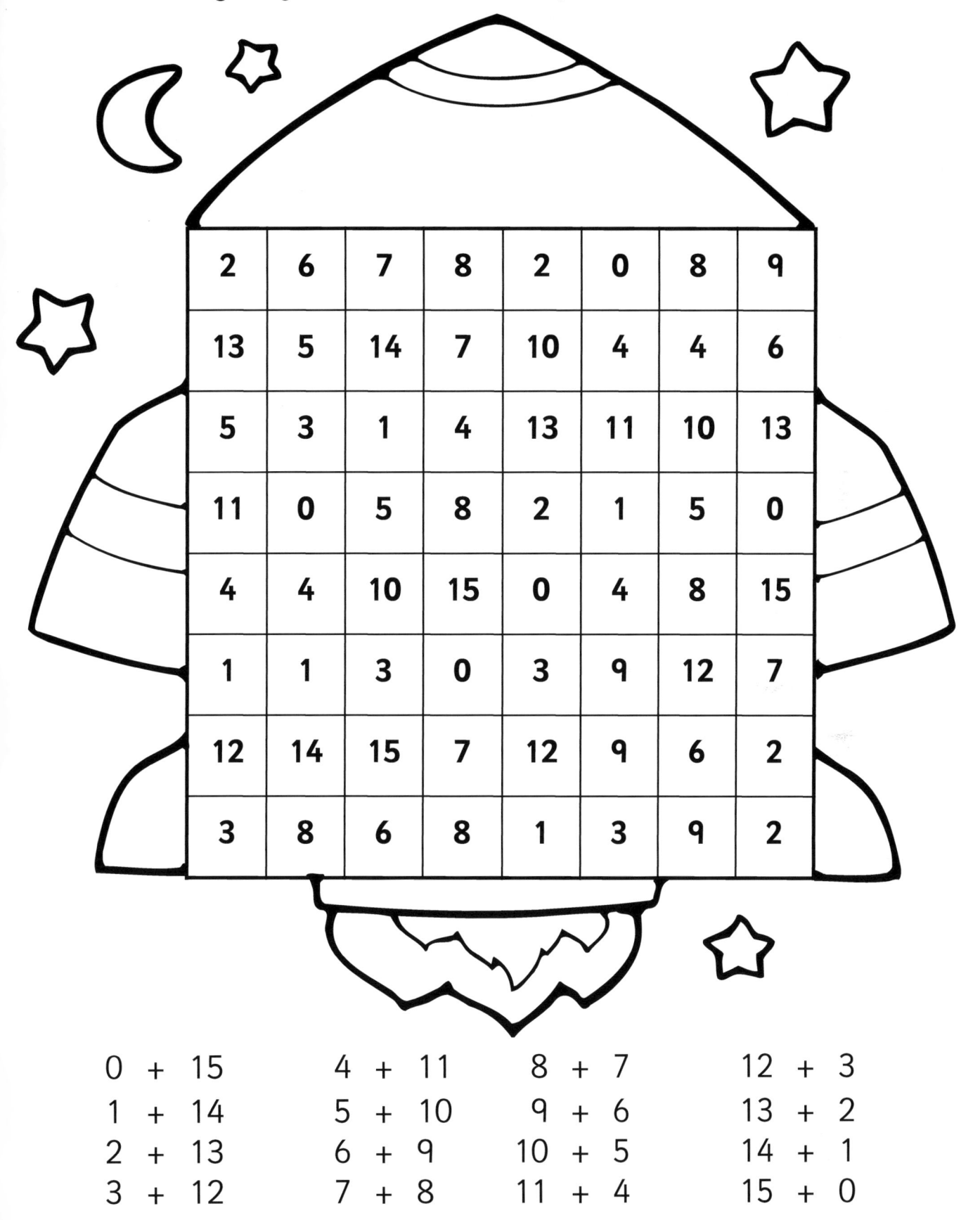

2	6	7	8	2	0	8	9
13	5	14	7	10	4	4	6
5	3	1	4	13	11	10	13
11	0	5	8	2	1	5	0
4	4	10	15	0	4	8	15
1	1	3	0	3	9	12	7
12	14	15	7	12	9	6	2
3	8	6	8	1	3	9	2

0 + 15   4 + 11   8 + 7   12 + 3
1 + 14   5 + 10   9 + 6   13 + 2
2 + 13   6 + 9   10 + 5   14 + 1
3 + 12   7 + 8   11 + 4   15 + 0

All bonds lie vertically in the grid.

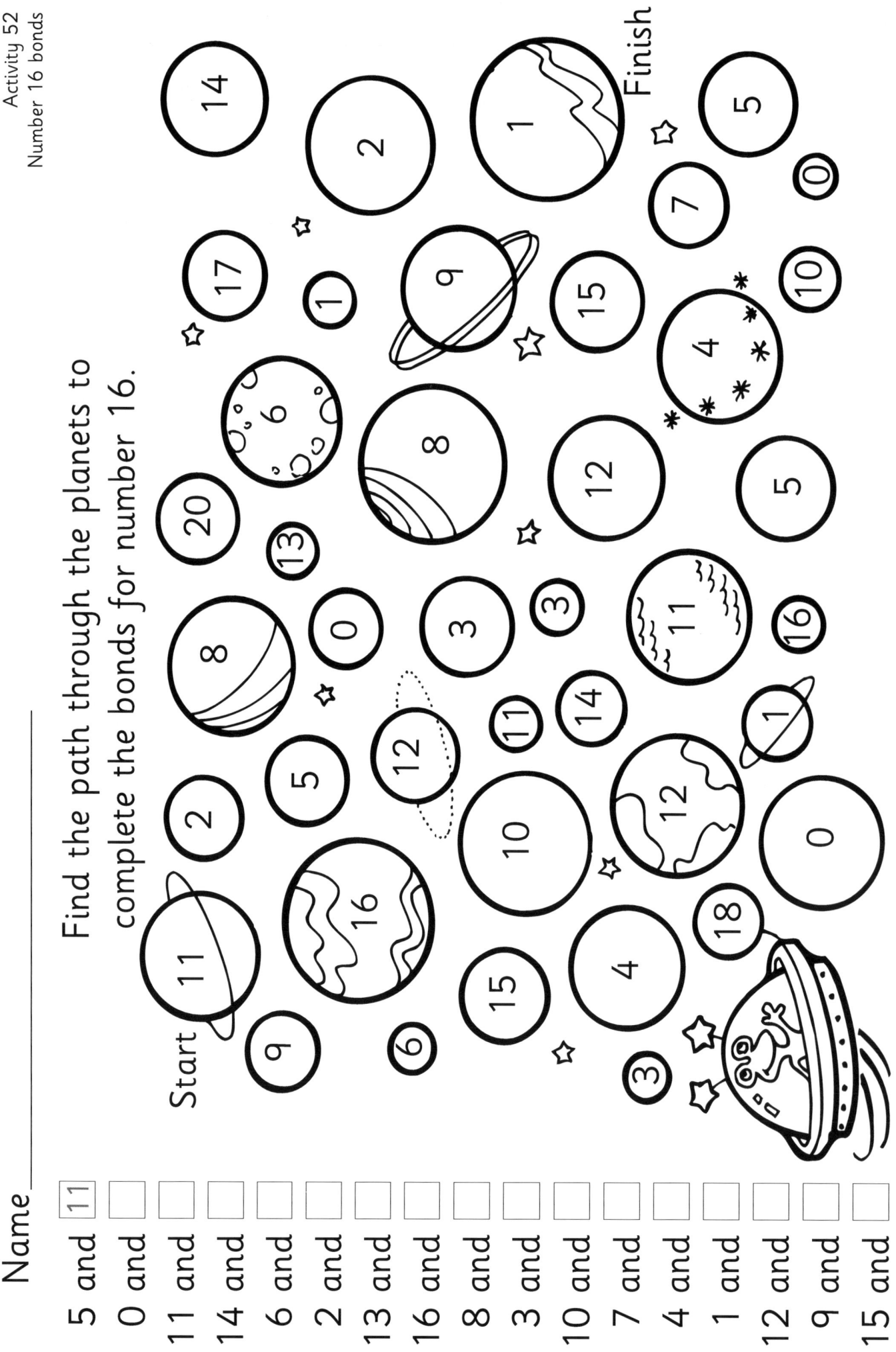

Activity 52
Number 16 bonds

Name _____

Find the path through the planets to complete the bonds for number 16.

5 and [11]
0 and □
11 and □
14 and □
6 and □
2 and □
13 and □
16 and □
8 and □
3 and □
10 and □
7 and □
4 and □
1 and □
12 and □
9 and □
15 and □

© Number Bonds Fun LDA

Name _____

Activity 53
Number 16 bonds

Use your number 16 bonds to colour match the tickets and machines.

63

© Number Bonds Fun LDA

Name _____

Activity 54
Number 17 bonds

Can you keep the plates spinning by finding the number 17 bond pairs?

- 12 / 6
- 11 / 5
- 5 / 12
- 13 / 6
- 0 / 17
- 4 / 13
- 8 / 8
- 3 / 14
- 7 / 7
- 1 / 16
- 8 / 9
- 9 / 5
- 10 / 5
- 6 / 11
- 2 / 15
- 7 / 10

Colour plates worth 17 blue and all other plates green.

© Number Bonds Fun LDA

Activity 55
Number 17 bonds

Name _____

Where is the treasure hidden?

9 and [8]
16 and [ ]
13 and [ ]
10 and [ ]
17 and [ ]
11 and [ ]
15 and [ ]
12 and [ ]
14 and [ ]

Use your number 17 bonds to find the hidden treasure.

© Number Bonds Fun LDA

Activity 56
Number 18 bonds

0 + 18
1 + 17
2 + 16
3 + 15
4 + 14
5 + 13
6 + 12
7 + 11
8 + 10
9 + 9
10 + 8
11 + 7
12 + 6
13 + 5
14 + 4
15 + 3
16 + 2
17 + 1
18 + 0

Name _____

Find the number bond pairs which make 18.

2	10	15	4	9	7	2	14	1
4	4	8	3	6	9	13	16	4
1	14	5	5	4	15	8	5	1
16	7	2	6	13	1	9	6	2
11	2	11	12	9	7	17	10	12
2	7	3	0	6	3	18	4	7
	0	5	8	0	3	8	0	
	4	18	17	10	2	15	3	
	3	9	1	10	8			

All bonds lie diagonally in the grid.

© Number Bonds Fun LDA

Name _____

Activity 57
Number 18 bonds

Use counters or cubes to find ways of making 18.
Write the number pairs on the pizzas.

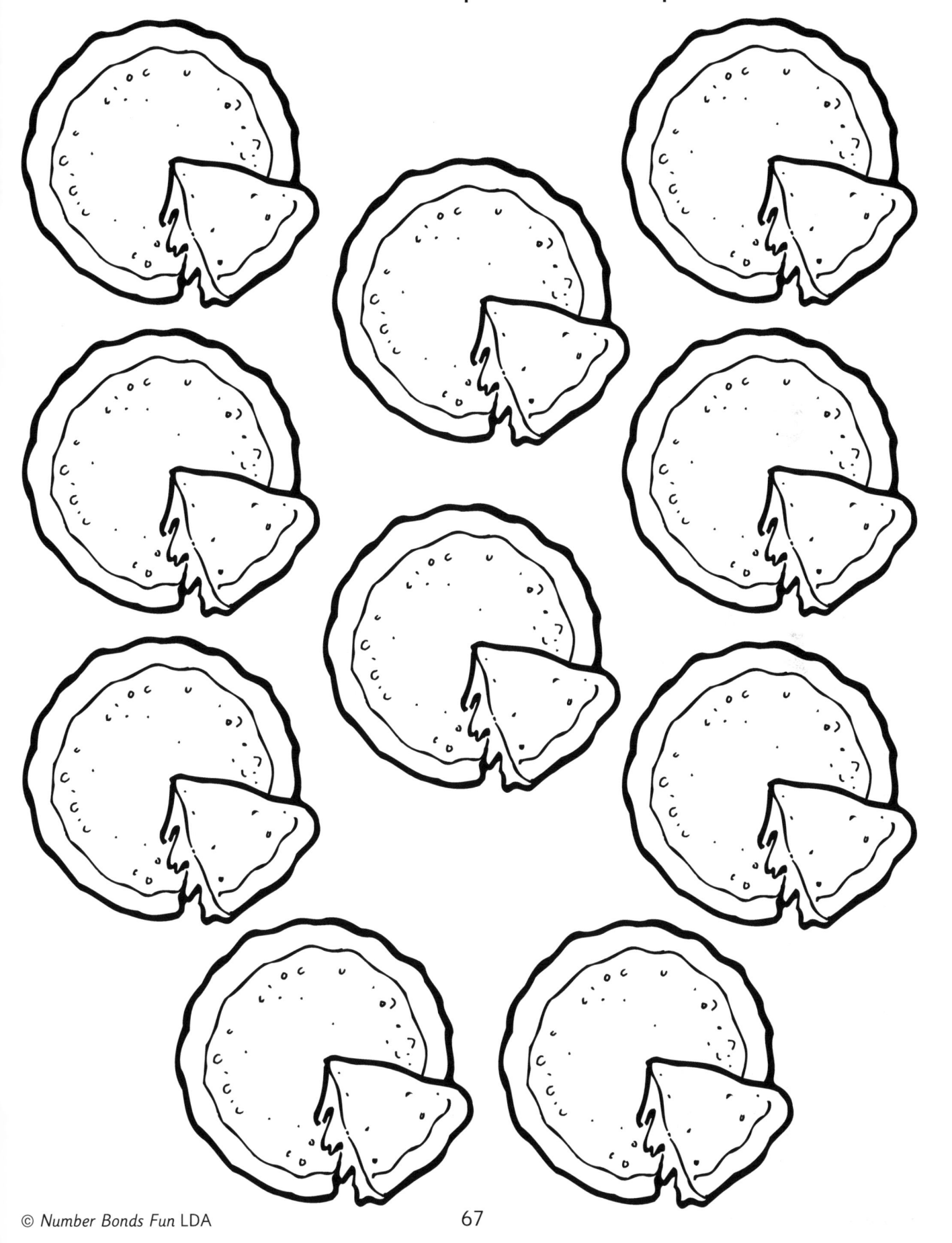

Name _____

Activity 58
Number 19 bonds

Colour match the number 19 bond bees.

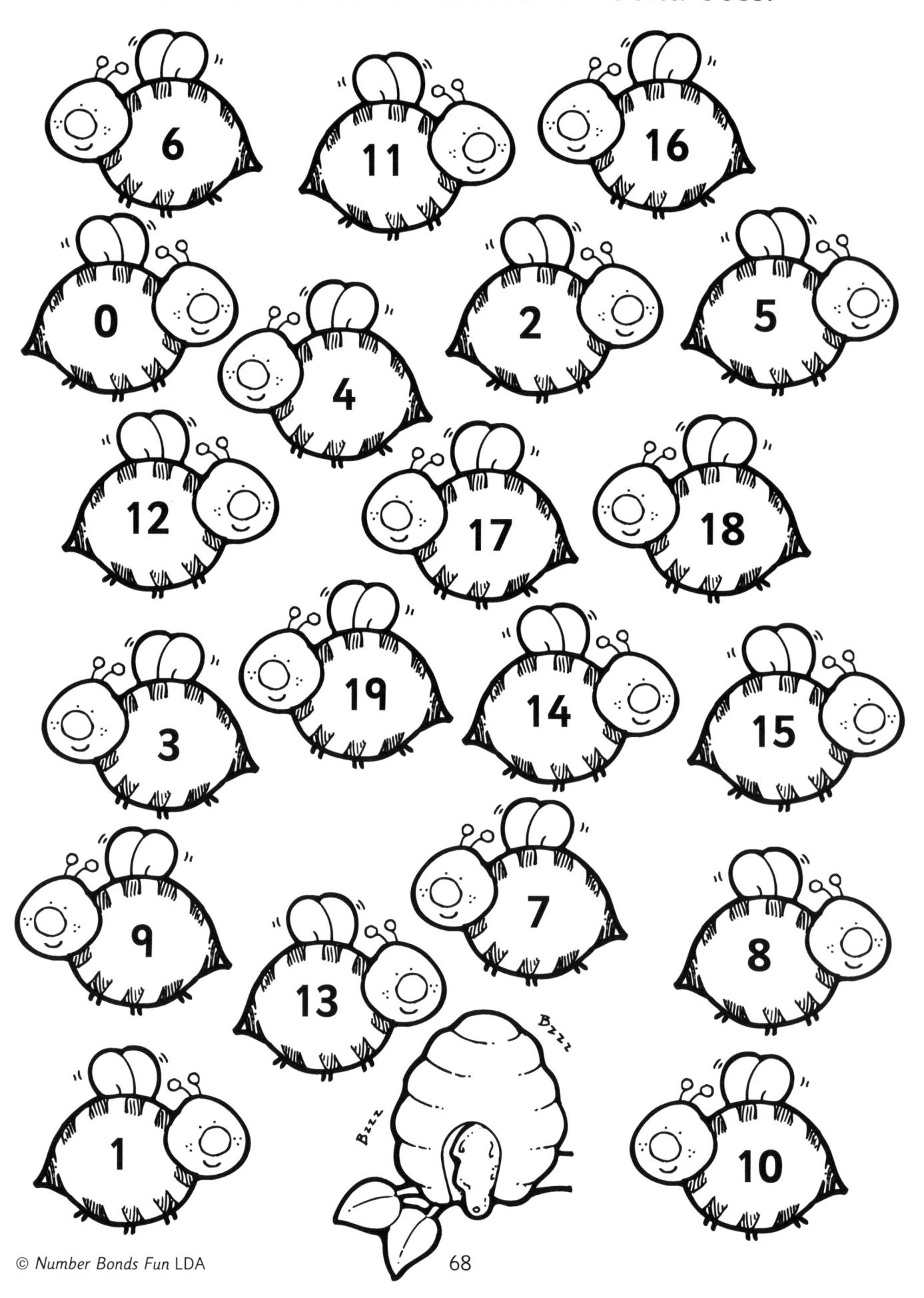

6 11 16
0 4 2 5
12 17 18
3 19 14 15
9 7 8
1 13 10

© Number Bonds Fun LDA

Name _____

Activity 59
Number 19 bonds

How many goals can you score? Find the hidden number 19 bond pairs. Colour balls totalling 19 orange, and all others blue.

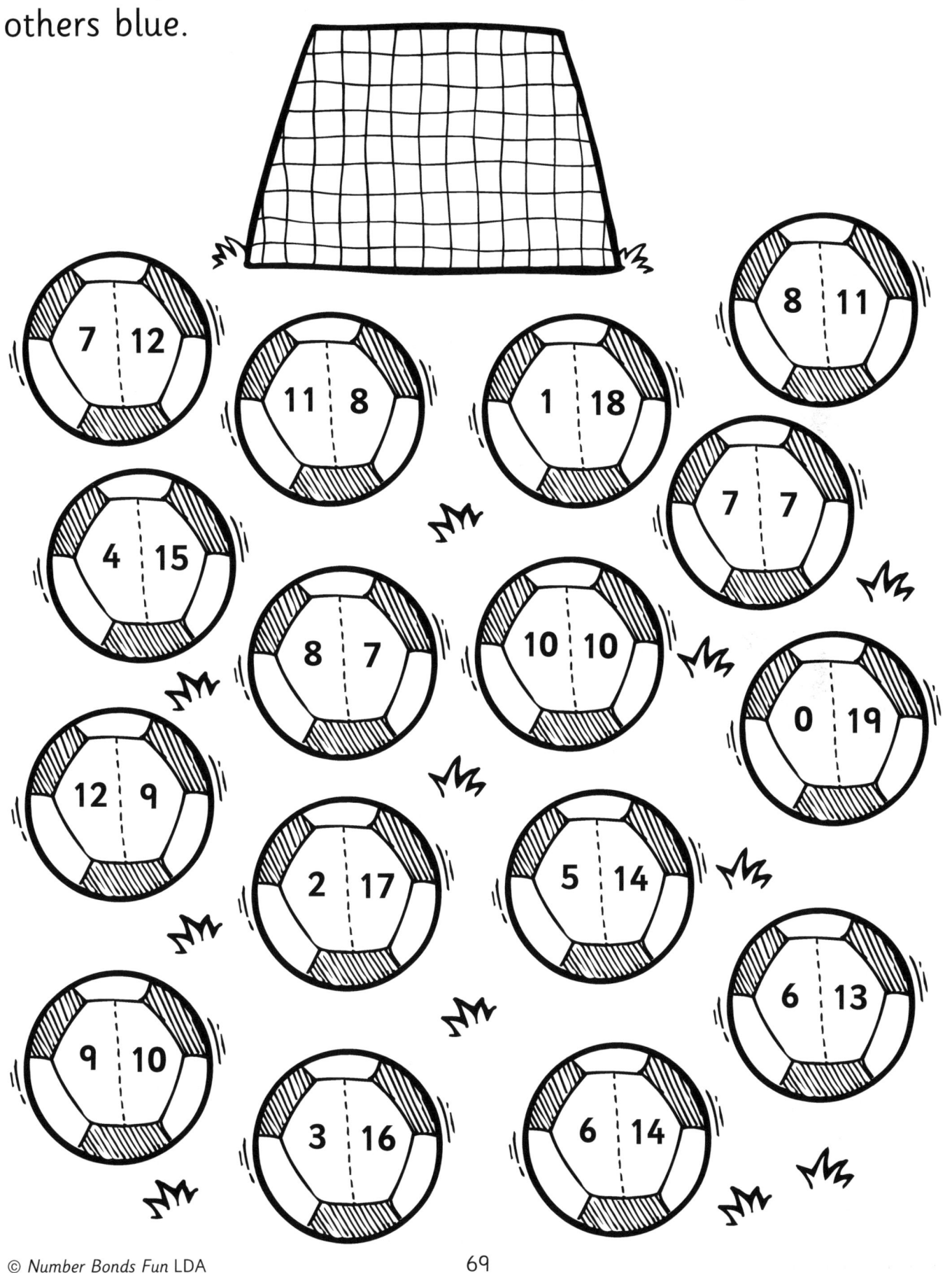

- 7 | 12
- 11 | 8
- 1 | 18
- 8 | 11
- 4 | 15
- 7 | 7
- 8 | 7
- 10 | 10
- 0 | 19
- 12 | 9
- 2 | 17
- 5 | 14
- 6 | 13
- 9 | 10
- 3 | 16
- 6 | 14

© Number Bonds Fun LDA
69

Name _____

Activity 60
Number 20 bonds

Every purse should have 20p. Can you add the missing money?

© Number Bonds Fun LDA
70

Name _____

Activity 61
Number 20 bonds

Follow the skipping ropes to find the bonds for number 20.

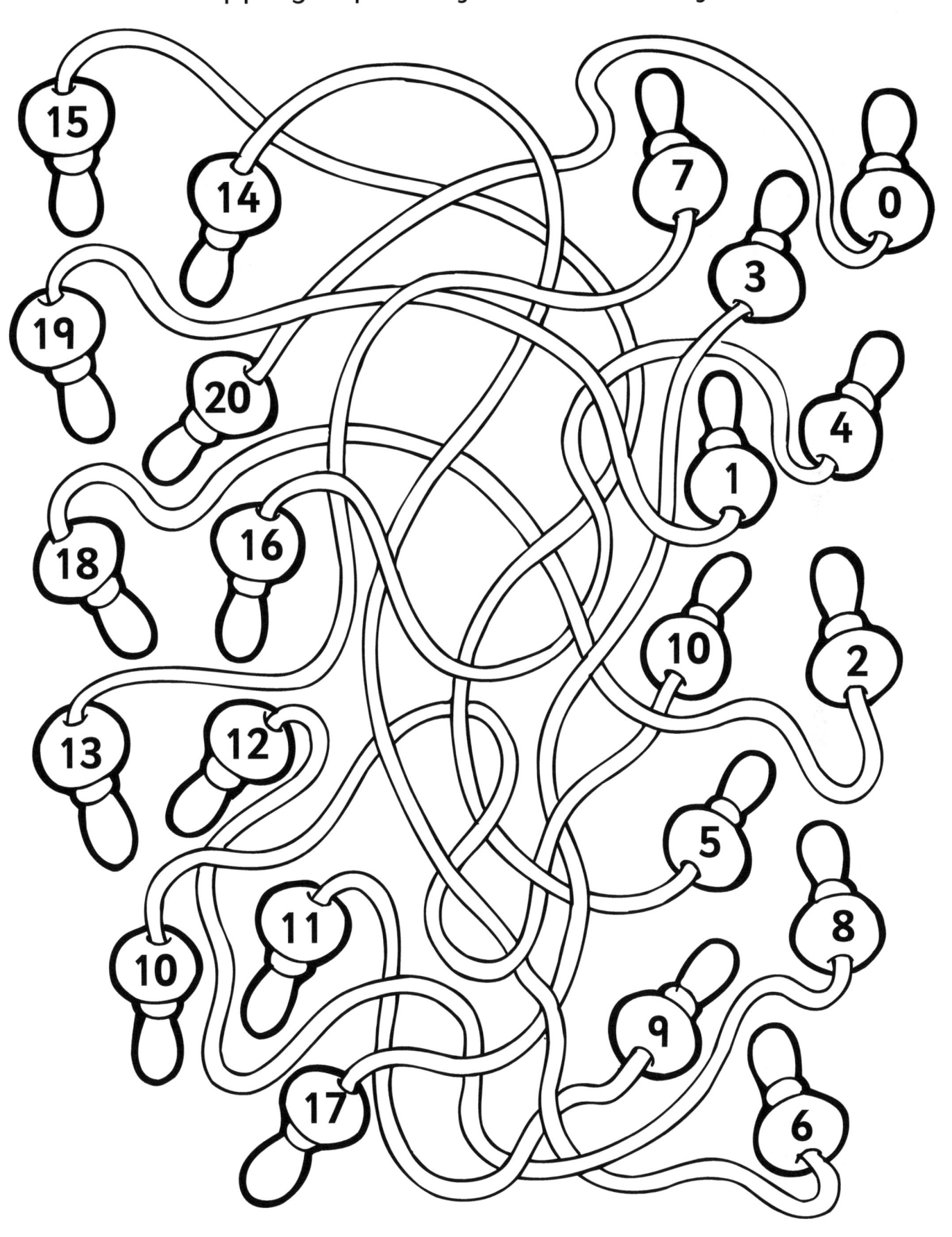

Colour each bond pair a different colour.

© Number Bonds Fun LDA

Name _____

Activity 62
Number 20 bonds

Number bond bees

8   5   1

6   3   7

2   0   4

10   9

© Number Bonds Fun LDA

Name _____   Activity 62
                              Number 20 bonds

Use your number bonds to match the bees to the flowers.

20   10
13   11
     14
15
   18   16
17 12   19

© Number Bonds Fun LDA   73

Name _____

Activity 63
Number 20 bonds

Can you find the missing number from each number 20 bond pair?

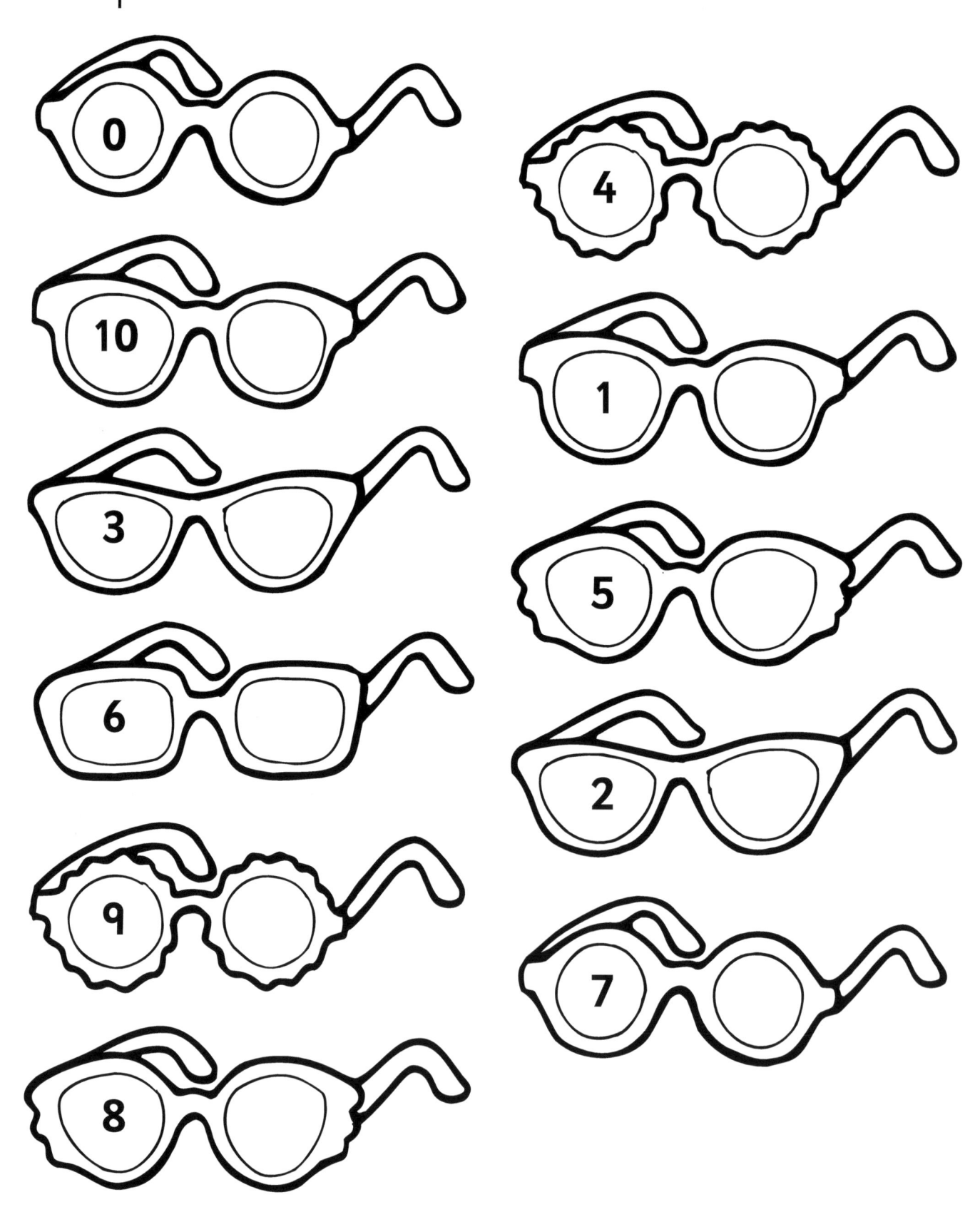

0

10

3

6

9

8

4

1

5

2

7

Colour each pair of glasses with a different colour.

© Number Bonds Fun LDA   74

Name _____

Activity 64
Number 20 bonds

Can you turn the number bond pairs around to find their friends? Colour the mittens so the pairs match.

0 and 20

20 and 0

8 and 12

7 and 13

1 and 19

9 and 11

10 and 10

2 and 18

6 and 14

4 and 16

3 and 17

5 and 15

© Number Bonds Fun LDA

75

Name _____

Activity 65
Number 20 bonds

Can you find the number bond pairs that make 20?

		10		4	0	3	
	20	10	15	20	19	1	5
10	0	11	5	6	14	4	2	6
9	13	7	20	8	0	10	10	18	19
14	12	4	16	12	0	5	15	7	16
6	1	18	20	17	3	1	16	9	4
20	19	11	6	9	11	12	8	11	3
8	7	9	0	20	13	20	3	2	
	13	20	17	18	2	15	17	
		1	14	0	9		

10 + 10
11 + 9
12 + 8
13 + 7
14 + 6

15 + 5
16 + 4
17 + 3
18 + 2
19 + 1
20 + 0

Don't forget that you can turn the numbers around. So 12 and 8 make 20 but 8 and 12 also make 20.

Name _____

Number bonds to twenty – hide and seek

10	11	12	13	14	15	16	17	18	19	20
10	9	8	7	6	5	4	3	2	1	0

Activity 66
Number 20 bonds

© Number Bonds Fun LDA

Name _____

Activity 67
Number 20 bonds

Make each pair of bananas total 20.

© Number Bonds Fun LDA

78

Name _____

Activity 68
Number 50 bonds

Colour match the submarines to make number bond pairs that equal 50.

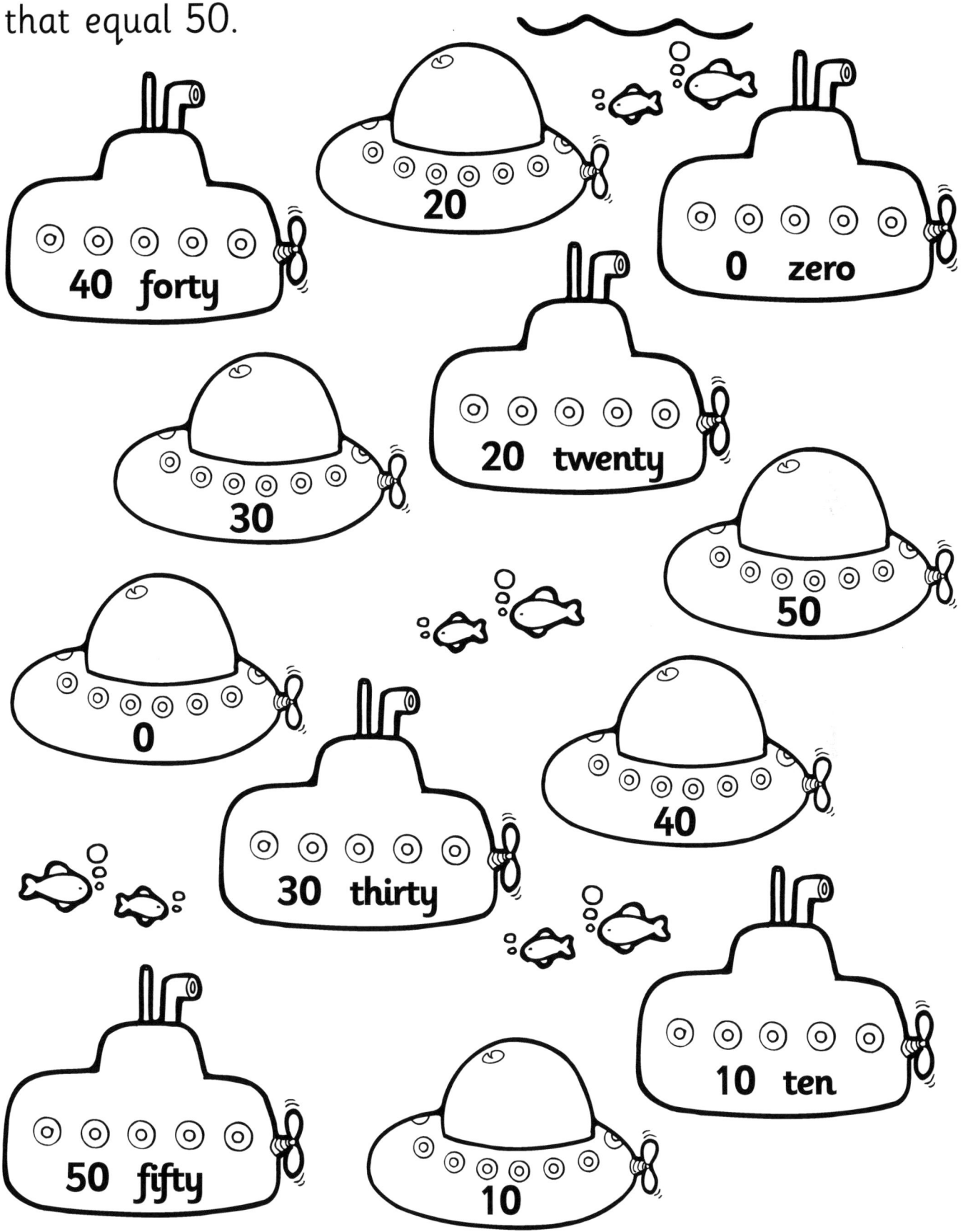

40 forty

20

0 zero

30

20 twenty

50

0

30 thirty

40

50 fifty

10

10 ten

Copy the number words onto the bubble submarines.

© Number Bonds Fun LDA

Name _____

Activity 69
Number 50 bonds

Cut and paste the t-shirts to make 50.

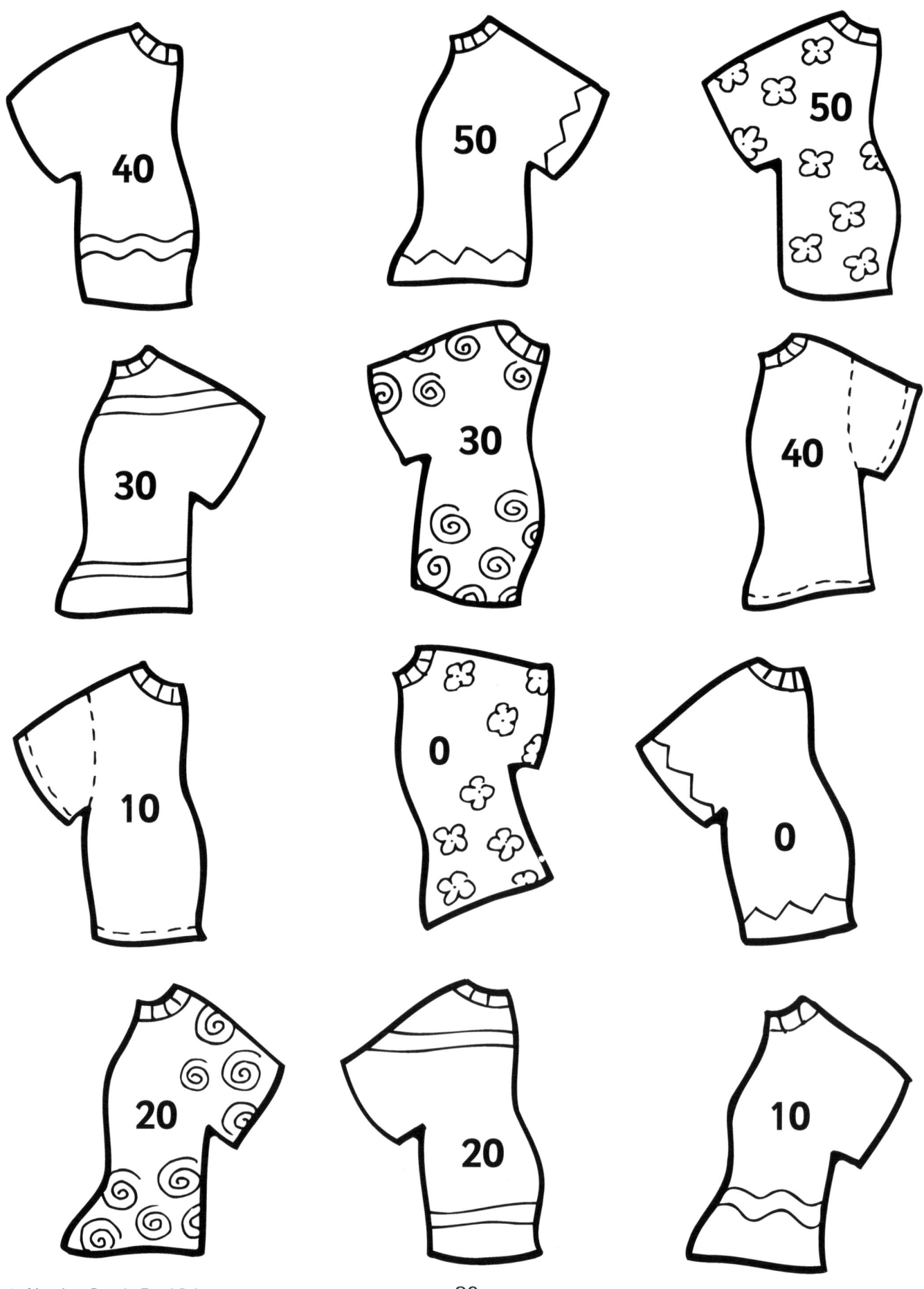

40   50   50

30   30   40

10   0   0

20   20   10

© Number Bonds Fun LDA   80

Name _____

Activity 70
Number 50 bonds

Each petal is worth 10. Can you work out how much is missing from each fifty flower?

Add the tens petals to the flowers and write the missing amount in the middle.

© Number Bonds Fun LDA

Name _____

Activity 71
Number 100 bonds

Follow the anchor ropes to find the bonds for 100.

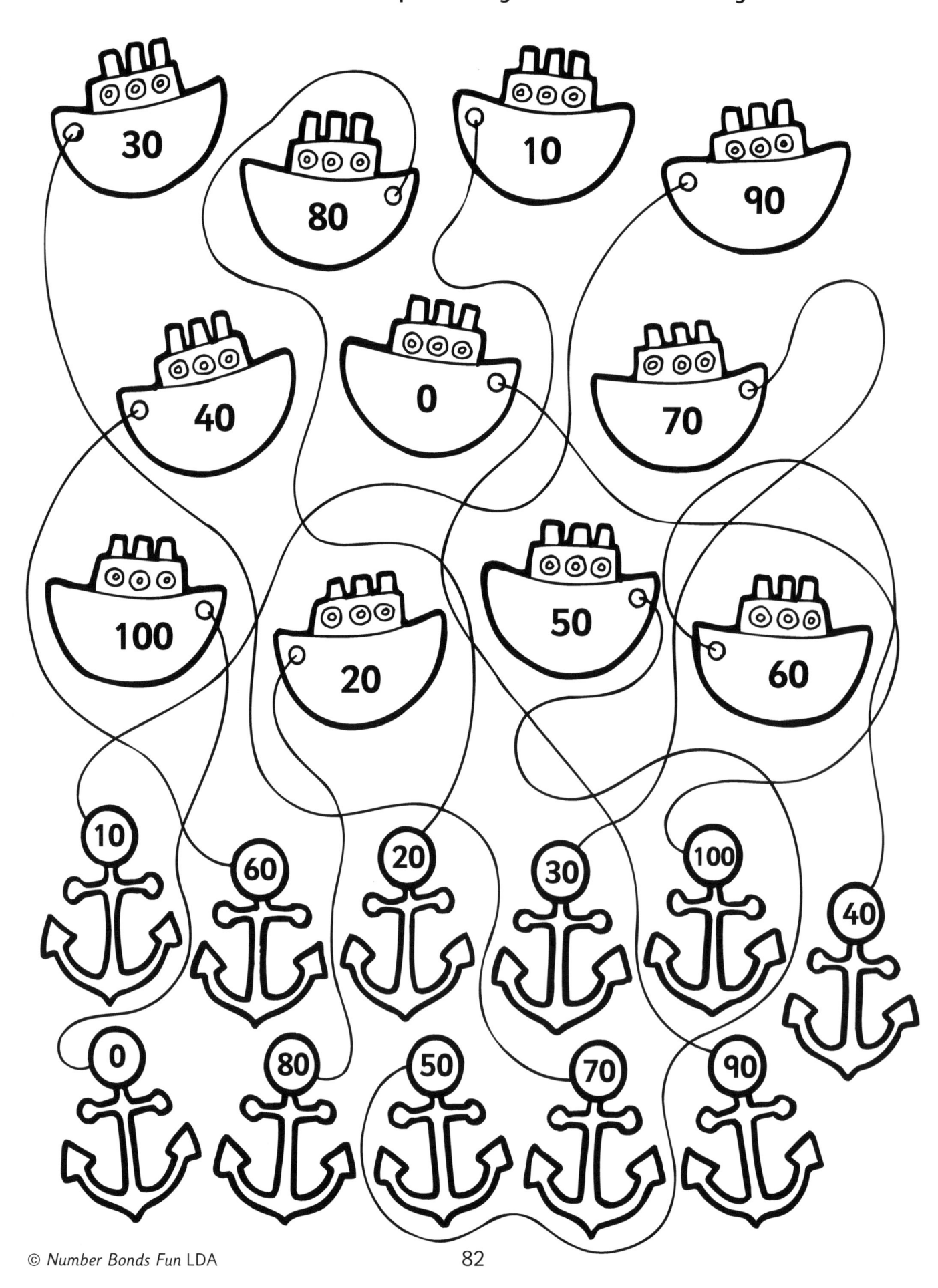

Boats: 30, 80, 10, 90, 40, 0, 70, 100, 20, 50, 60

Anchors: 10, 60, 20, 30, 100, 40, 0, 80, 50, 70, 90

© Number Bonds Fun LDA

Name _____

Activity 72
Number 100 bonds

Colour match the cannons to the cannonballs by making

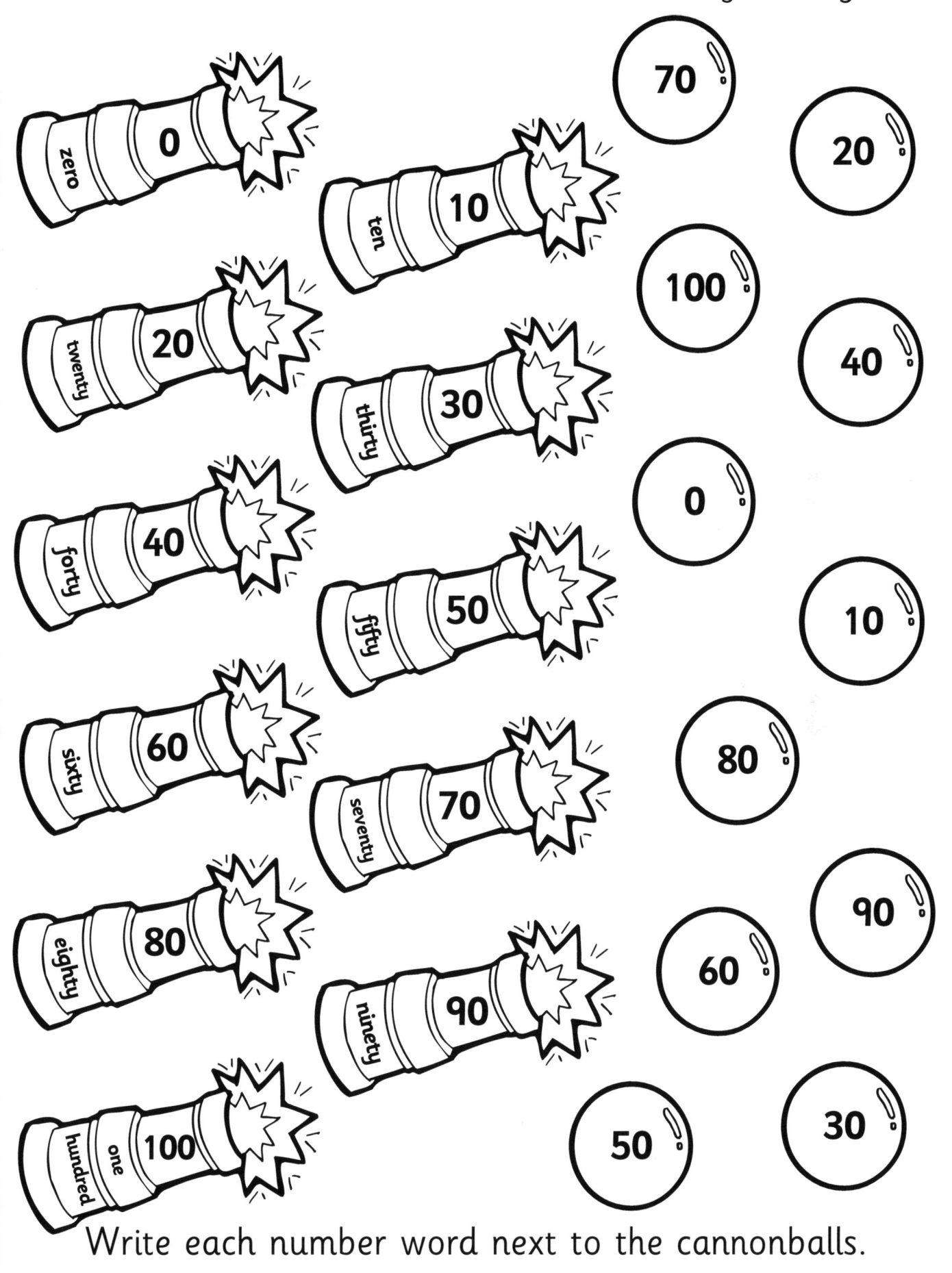

Write each number word next to the cannonballs.

© Number Bonds Fun LDA

Name _____

Activity 73
Number 100 bonds

Write the matching number 100 bond on the opposite snake. Colour each pair a different colour.

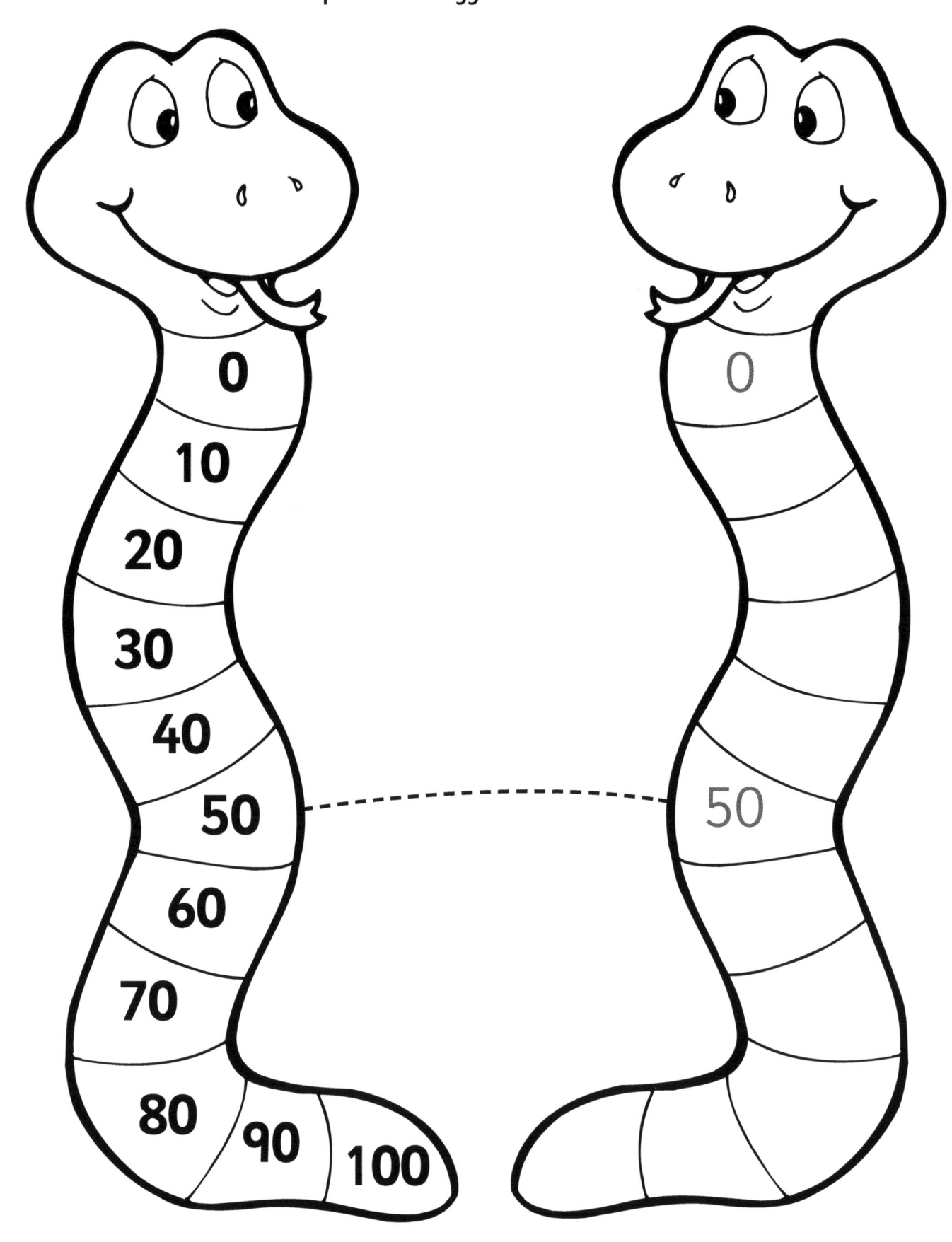

Left snake: 0, 10, 20, 30, 40, 50, 60, 70, 80, 90, 100

Right snake: 0, 50

© Number Bonds Fun LDA

Name _____ Activity 74
Number 100 bonds

Cut out the strips and use your number 100 bonds to put the alien back together.

	60 and 40
	100 and 0
	0 and 100
	30 and 70
	80 and 20
	20 and 80
	50 and 50
	40 and 60
	90 and 10
	70 and 30
	10 and 90

© Number Bonds Fun LDA

Name _____

Activity 75
Number 100 bonds

Cut out the cracker halves. Use your number 100 bonds to help you join the correct cracker halves together.

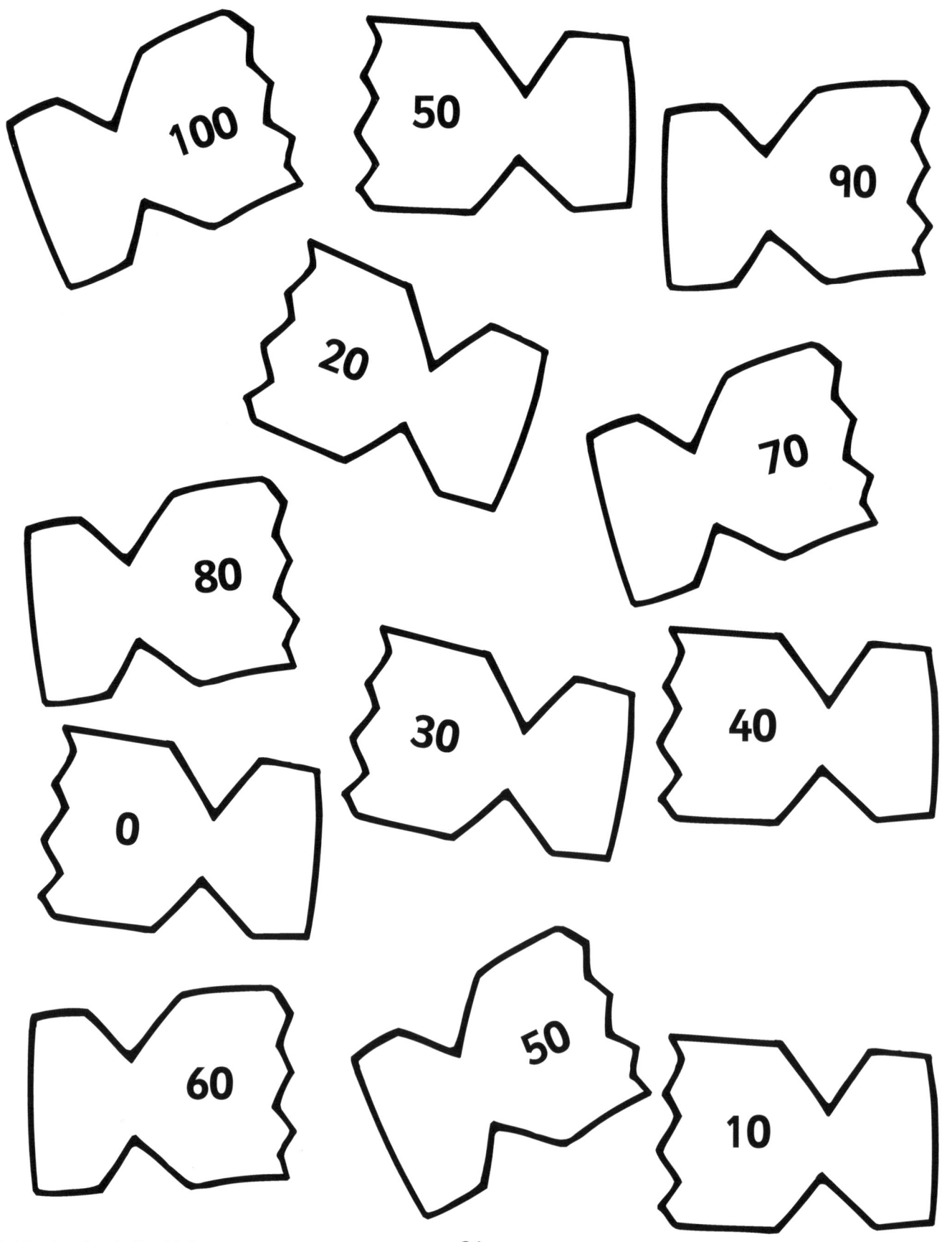

100 50 90

20 70

80

30 40

0

60 50 10

© Number Bonds Fun LDA

Name _____

Activity 76
Number 100 bonds

Number bond rockets for use with Number 100 bond rocket lotto.

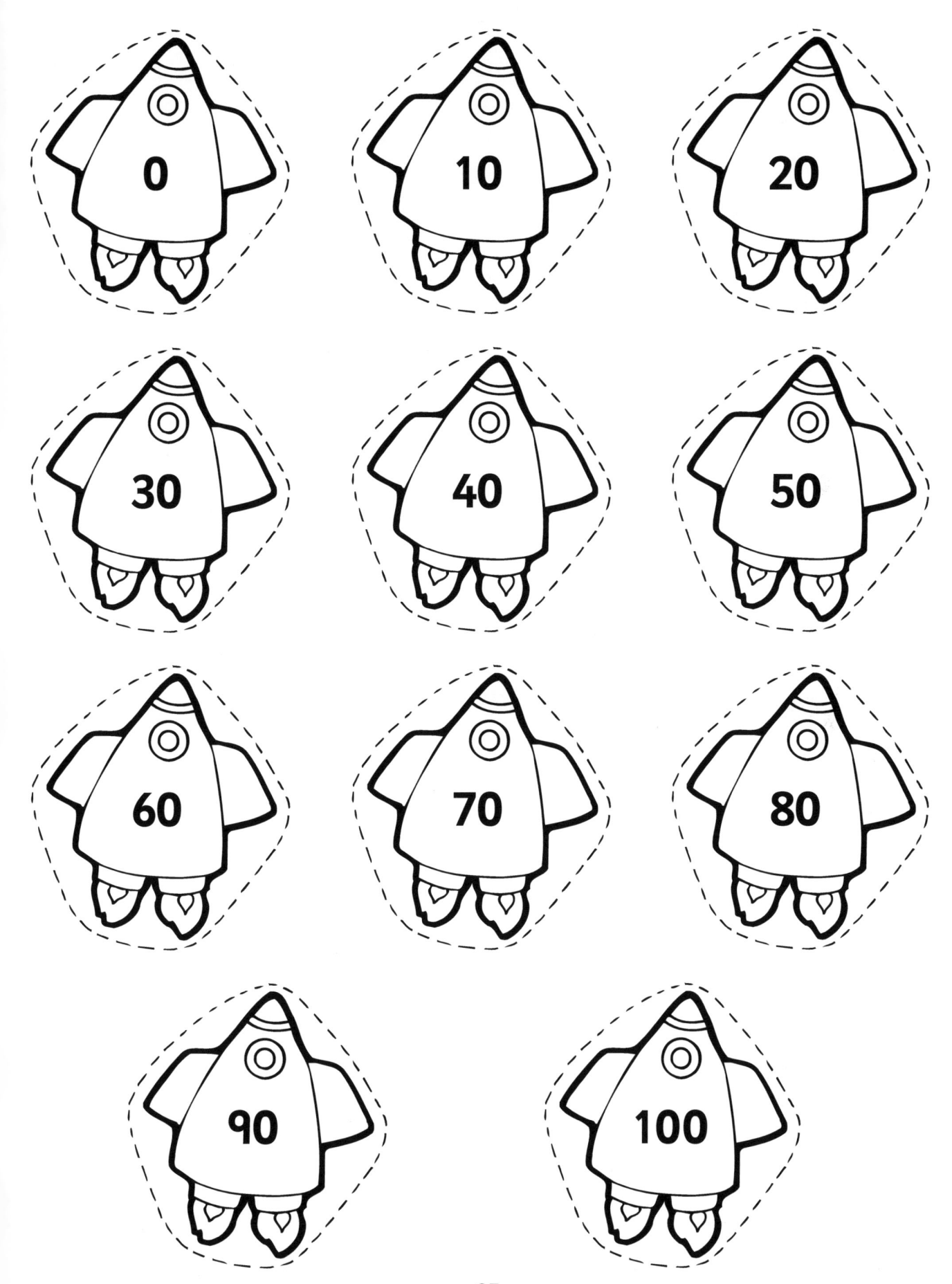

0 10 20

30 40 50

60 70 80

90 100

© Number Bonds Fun LDA

Name _____

Activity 76
Number 100 bonds

Use your number 100 bonds to help you match the rockets to the planets.

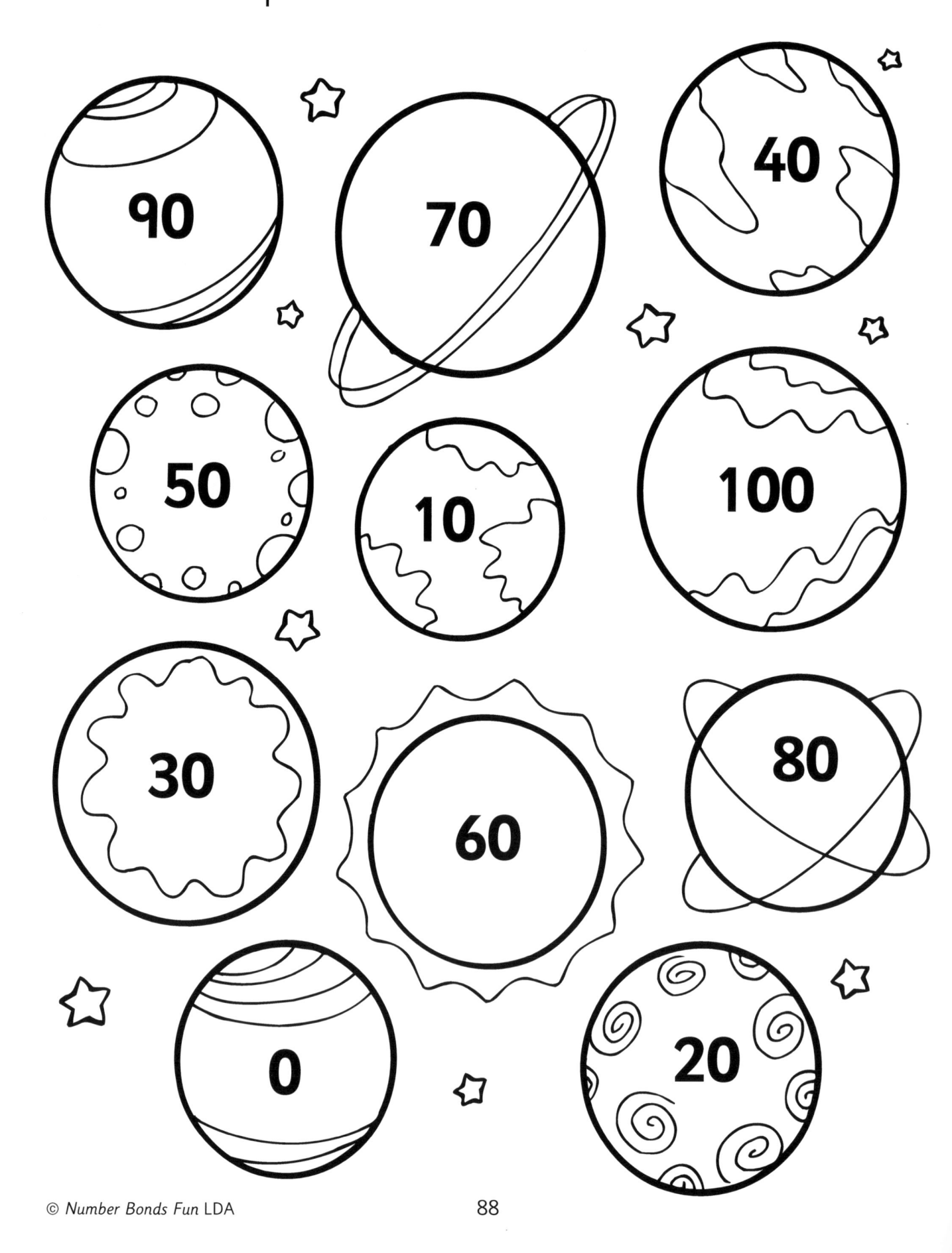

90   70   40

50   10   100

30   60   80

0   20

© Number Bonds Fun LDA

Name _____

Activity 77
Mixed number bonds to 20

Racing car lotto bonds

5 4	8 8	5 1
9 8	11 2	6 5
5 10	3 2	10 4
4 3	3 9	2 6
7 3	16 4	18 1
	9 9	

© Number Bonds Fun LDA

Name _____

Activity 77
Mixed number bonds to 20

Winners badges

5	6	7
8	9	10
11	12	13
14	15	16
17	18	20
	19	

© Number Bonds Fun LDA

Name _____

Activity 78
Mixed number bonds

Number bond addition square

+	0	1	2	3	4	5	6	7	8	9	10
0											
1											
2											
3											
4											
5											
6											
7											
8											
9											
10											

Complete the square. Have you noticed any patterns?

© Number Bonds Fun LDA

Name _____

Activity 79
Mixed number bonds

Write number bond pairs on each door that total the number on the lorries.

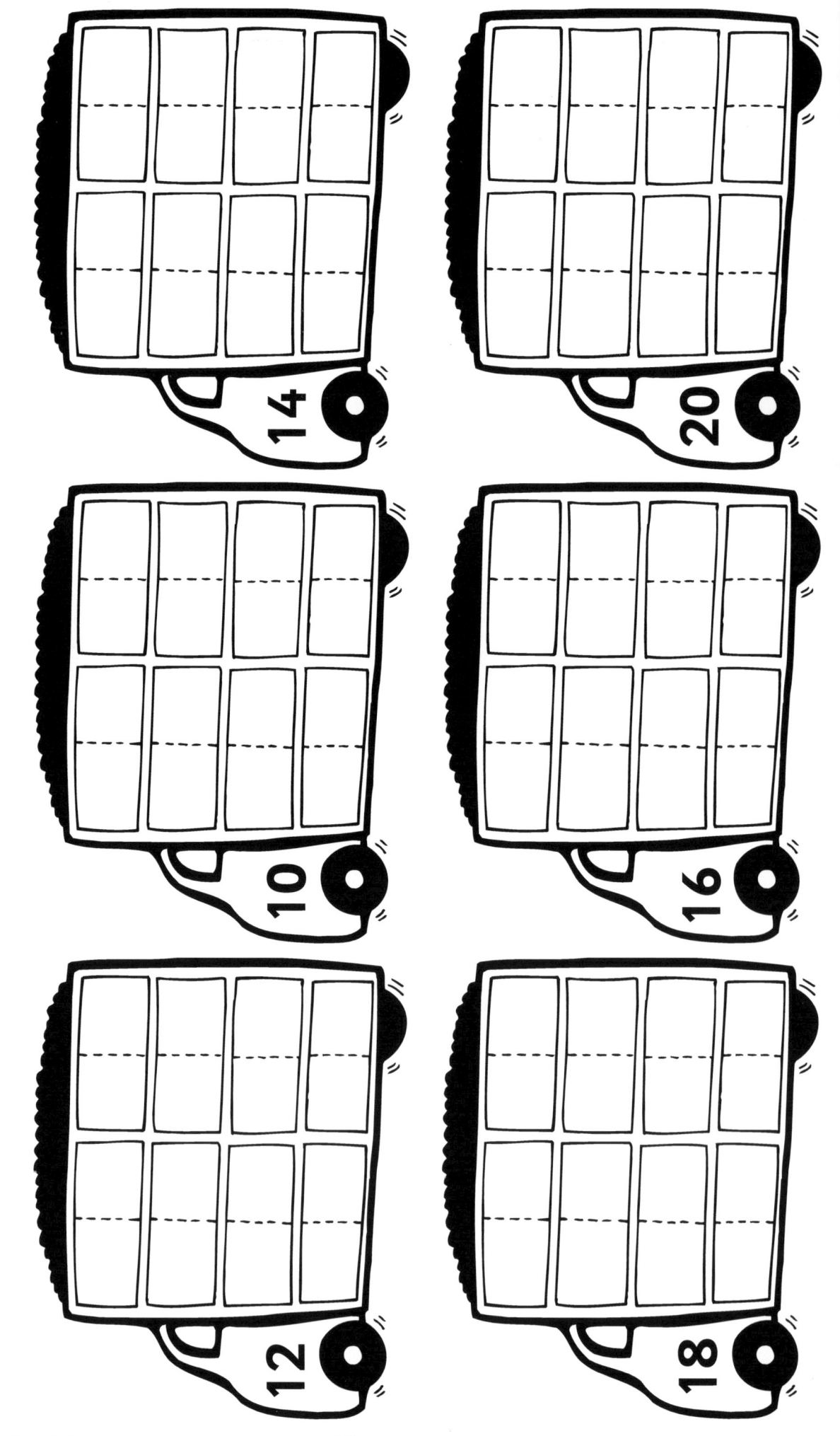

12

10

14

18

16

20

© Number Bonds Fun LDA

Name _____

Activity 80
Mixed number bonds

Journey to the bottom of the sea

Start

2 and 0
3 and 4
1 and 1
6 and 1
5 and 1
2 and 6
0 and 4
1 and 3
5 and 5
7 and 2
0 and 10
4 and 6
0 and 0
3 and 5
8 and 1
5 and 2
4 and 4
7 and 1
0 and 5
2 and 4
4 and 5
2 and 8
1 and 0
3 and 2
1 and 6
3 and 7
4 and 2
6 and 3
2 and 2
2 and 7
4 and 1
6 and 4
5 and 3
0 and 8
7 and 3
0 and 9
3 and 0
5 and 4
5 and 0
2 and 3
3 and 6
10 and 0
6 and 0
3 and 3
0 and 7
2 and 1
9 and 0
0 and 0
0 and 8

Finish

© Number Bonds Fun LDA

Name _____   Activity 81
                                               Mixed number bonds

Journey to the bottom of the sea

Start

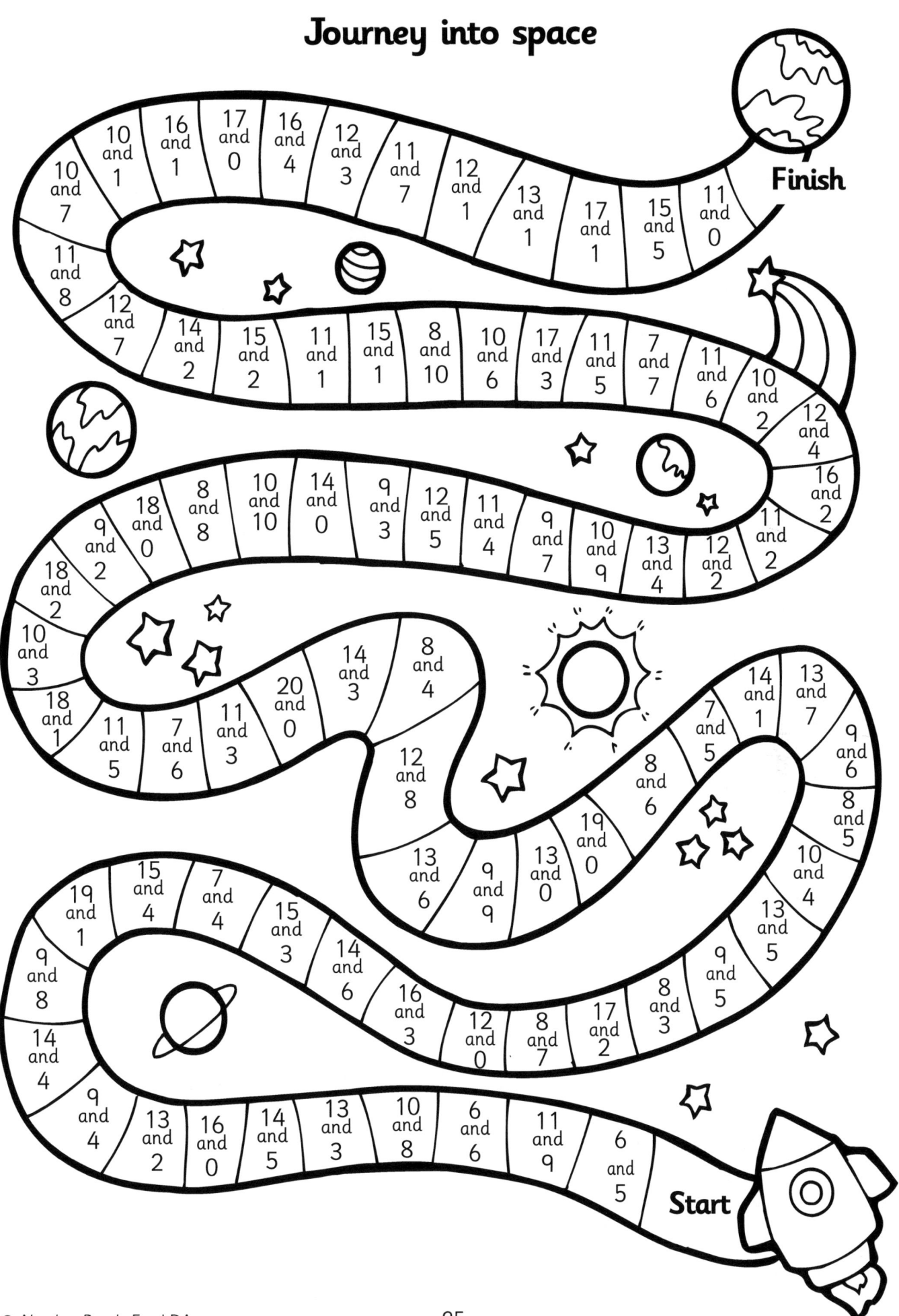

Name _____

Activity 82
Mixed number bonds

Journey into space

A winding board game path from "Start" (bottom right, near a rocket) to "Finish" (top right, near a planet), with each segment containing a number bond pair:

Starting from Start:
6 and 5, 11 and 9, 6 and 6, 10 and 8, 13 and 3, 14 and 5, 16 and 0, 13 and 2, 9 and 4, 14 and 4, 9 and 8, 19 and 1, 15 and 4, 7 and 4, 15 and 3, 14 and 6, 16 and 3, 12 and 0, 8 and 7, 17 and 2, 8 and 3, 9 and 5, 13 and 5, 10 and 4, 8 and 5, 9 and 6, 13 and 7, 14 and 1, 7 and 5, 8 and 6, 19 and 0, 13 and 0, 9 and 9, 13 and 6, 12 and 8, 8 and 4, 14 and 3, 20 and 0, 11 and 3, 7 and 6, 11 and 5, 18 and 1, 10 and 3, 18 and 2, 9 and 2, 8 and 0, 10 and 10, 14 and 0, 9 and 3, 12 and 5, 11 and 4, 9 and 7, 10 and 9, 13 and 4, 12 and 2, 11 and 2, 16 and 2, 12 and 4, 10 and 2, 11 and 6, 7 and 7, 11 and 5, 17 and 3, 10 and 6, 8 and 10, 15 and 1, 11 and 1, 15 and 2, 14 and 2, 12 and 7, 11 and 8, 10 and 7, 16 and 1, 17 and 0, 16 and 4, 12 and 3, 11 and 7, 12 and 1, 13 and 1, 17 and 1, 15 and 5, 11 and 0

Finish

© Number Bonds Fun LDA

95

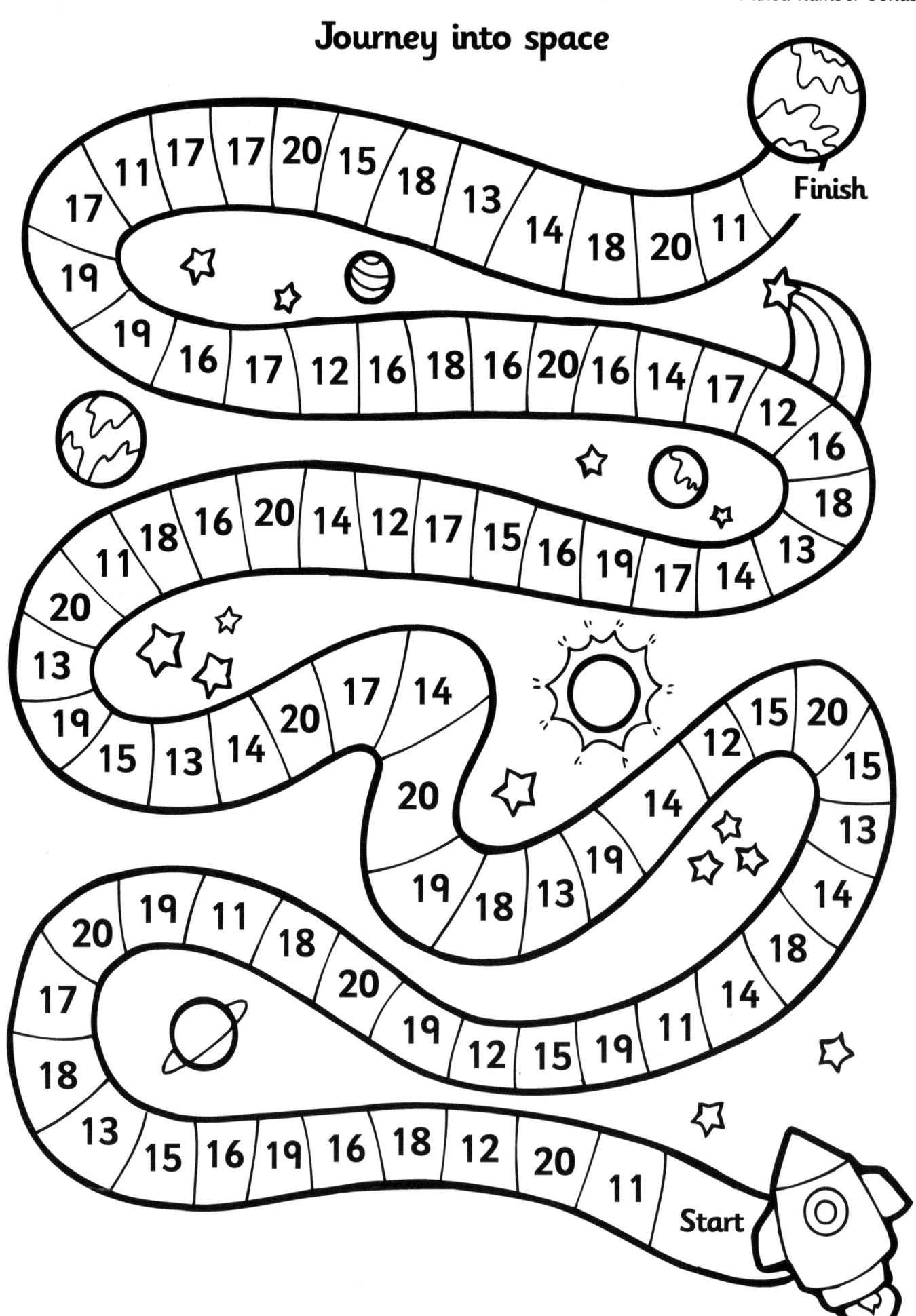

Name _____

Activity 83
Mixed number bonds

Journey into space

© Number Bonds Fun LDA